⋎ **W9-BHS-186**

Nashville
Public Library
Foundation

*This book
made possible
through generous gifts
to the
Nashville Public Library
Foundation Book Fund*

it!

# it!

## 9 Secrets of the
## Rich and Famous
## That Will Take You to the Top

# Paula Froelich

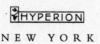

miramax books

HYPERION

NEW YORK

Copyright © 2005 Paula Froelich

All rights reserved. No part of this book may be used
or reproduced in any manner whatsoever without
the written permission of the Publisher.
Printed in the United States of America.
For information address
Hyperion, 77 West 66th Street, New York, NY 10023-6298

ISBN 1-4013-5210-3

First Edition
10   9   8   7   6   5   4   3   2   1

# Contents

# it!

## Introduction

# Starting Off

WHAT IS FAME? WHY DO PEOPLE WANT TO BE FAMOUS? What's the difference between being famous and being notorious? Does the distinction even matter anymore? How come some people seem to be born popular, beautiful, and fabulous, while the rest of us are seemingly left to rot in obscurity? Why does one person get to become an "expert" on TV, when you know you can do a better job?

I work for the *New York Post*'s "Page Six" gossip section, which means I am faced with these questions, either from myself or from others calling in daily. I am busy, along with my colleague Chris Wilson and my boss Richard Johnson, deciding who is famous enough to warrant mention in our column and who is hot enough to merit coronation on Page Six, which may gain them admittance into that highly exclusive club of boldfaced names. We decide who is interesting enough to merit mention, and sometimes it isn't just the obvious.

But one thing I have learned, during my time at Page Six, is that stars are made and not born. There is a whole machine behind every single person—whether it is a team of people or the person runs that machine on their own. There are rules to this fame game and everyone should know them. Why? Because if you are bold enough to take your career or business to the next level, you can become successful beyond your wildest dreams. In fact, you can attain any level of success you want in any field by following the lessons I lay out in this book.

Since "Page Six" germinates a lot of the stories that national magazines and newspapers pick up and follow, I am on the ground floor with a bird's-eye view of how stars are made. On a typical day, my phone rings hundreds of times. My e-mail in-box is off the charts. The tone of those correspondents varies from calm and professional to desperate and deranged. There is the PR person who will lose their job if I don't agree to cover their event. There is my mother. There is a trusted source with a "spotting" of a famous movie star making out with a famous rock star at the club Cabana. There is the person from the publicity department of a film company who wants coverage of a movie premiere, and promises that Elvis Presley will be in attendance at the after-party. There is the head of a talent agency calling to dish about a rival, or the music company executive calling to brag about his latest acquisition. And then there is always the PR person who's gotten wind of a client's forthcoming mention in my column, and wants me to kill the item because their client doesn't want to be "overexposed."

Eighty percent of my e-mail and phone calls are from publicists with an item, or at least what they hope I will decide is juicy enough to become an item. The best publicists know ahead of time what I want and when I want it. They know what they will have to come through with in the future (Gwyneth has ditched Chris, and Brad has ditched Jennifer, and they are back together!) in order for me to consider using a far less exciting (read: dull as dirt) item on their once-famous client no one has heard from in the last three years (although in the brutal world I inhabit, the top publicists have probably dumped that client already). It may sound harsh, but let's face it: An ad opposite Page Six can run you $30,000, so an item better be worth its weight in gold.

What do I have to offer you, if you are not dating Tom Cruise, do not have a starring role in the latest major motion picture, or have not appeared in a homemade porn film with Paris Hilton?

There have been countless times when I have run an item in Page Six because the pitch is interesting, the person has really done his or her homework in terms of what works as an item, and I have a sense that while the subjects might not be *People* magazine cover material yet, they are hot, on the verge, up and coming. I will take a chance on that kind of person. And I will show you in this book how to maximize your chances to make that kind of success for yourself.

But first let me tell you what you are up against in terms of the front lines of gossip reporting. The other day at Page Six I was doing what I usually do around deadline time—that is, checking facts on stories, fielding questions from my boss/editor, Richard, and banging out a few e-mails—when the phones exploded. It was 4:30 P.M., and we have to have our stories in by 5:30 or we get yelled at by Richard's boss, Steve "the crustaceous man" Cuozzo, who always has a complete loss of humor at this time of day, especially when he is also trying to finish writing his real estate column, which coincidentally that day he was.

**Call #1, 4:30 P.M.:** "Hey, so this is [publicist]. I'm calling from [firm], and I just wanted to see if you got our fax about the party we are having for this charity Thursday night and if you'll be coming." (My answer: I did not get the fax, I don't know if I'm coming, and won't decide until the night of. Thank you. I am on deadline.)

**Call #2, 4:35 P.M.:** (from really annoying PR woman who ends every sentence in a question): "Hi? So, um, I've got this rilly cute item? Angie Everhart was at this party for Michael Kors's new fragrance and she walked right up to Michael and said, um, 'Hey, where did you get your shirt?' Get it? Isn't that funny? I mean, she was talking to Michael Kors, and it was a Michael Kors shirt. Can you put it in the paper?" (My answer, a little less politely than last time: Okay, number one I hate the word *cute*, and number two, no, it is a retarded item!)

**Call #3, 4:37 P.M.:** "Hi. I'm calling from [firm] and we want to break something with you exclusively." (Yes, what?, slightly eagerly.) "On Thursday, Sarah Jessica Parker will be at Macy's unveiling the new diamante collection." (So what?) "Well, we haven't told anyone else." (That's because no one cares!) End of call.

**Call #4, 4:41 P.M.:** "Dude, it's [party promoter]. I just heard Gwyneth Paltrow got married today at [place]." (My answer, and this time I am excited: Thanks. You rock. I'll check it out.) "Cool, but can you get something else in the column for me? My client is on my ass . . ." (Now I'm suspicious, but I ask what the item is. It's a lame item, I knew it. PR person is still pushing though, and now I owe her for the Gwyneth item, which in the end was true. The item was lame, but quid pro quo . . . )

**Call #5, 4:46 P.M.:** "Paula, it's your mother." (My answer, the universal: Mom, I can't talk now . . . ) And the universal mom response: "You can never talk. You're always on deadline. You're always busy. I could die and—" (Mom, can I call you back later . . . ? Please?)

4:50 P.M.: Quick smoke break outside. How many mother-inspired guilt trips have resulted in need for cigarette?

**Call #6, 5:00 P.M.:** "Hi. I'm calling from [PR company] and we are updating our records. Do you have a moment to verify some information?" (My answer: *click*.)

**Call #7, 5:05 P.M.:** "Hi. Can I send you an e-mail?" (Can I stop you?)

**Call #8, 5:12 P.M.:** "Hello. I own a restaurant on Bond Street and I just wanted to let you know that Ethan Hawke and his new girlfriend were in here last night and they were all over each other." (My answer: Great. Can you send me an e-mail? Let me get your number. I am on deadline but I promise to get back to you tomorrow.)

**Call #9, 5:15 P.M.:** "Hi Paula. It's [PR person]. So I checked into that matter for you. Debra Messing wasn't even in New York on that day, so she couldn't have been at the bar dancing on the tables wearing no underwear. And with three eighteen-year-old guys? She's been in Yugoslavia all month shooting a beer commercial." (My answer: Sigh. Drop item.)

**Call #10, 5:20 P.M.:** "This is Wayne from Brooklyn and I just want to say I have been a loyal reader of the *Post* for ten years but I'm canceling my subscription. Stop bashing Michael Jackson! When he slept with those boys he was just being paternal!!" Phone slams in my ear.

7

Believe it or not, I made my deadline that day. I usually do, but it's almost always a close call. Almost every day, my phone rings constantly, and what usually distinguishes one call from another is that, while most of the calls are from public relations people selling "product," some are good at it and some are not. What is the moral of the story? If I don't want my time wasted by someone who is ill prepared, doesn't know a good item from a bad one, doesn't know how to present their story effectively, and therefore does not achieve the desired result, then I guarantee you that wherever you live, whatever your profession, whatever you are trying to sell, whatever job you are trying to get, you have to learn how to do it right, and that's just what I'm going to teach you.

## Chapter One

# The Rules of Fame
## (and How They Can
## Make You a Success)

ADMIT IT. YOU HAVE AT LEAST ONCE IN YOUR LIFE FAN-tasized about being that intriguing, charismatic person with that ineffable star quality who walks into a room and all heads turn. The "it" person.

For many, this is a dream that begins and ends in junior high school. For others, it is a daydream that gets honed through high school and college, and then after, into an actual ambition, a goal. But often it doesn't get translated into a plan, mainly because the daydreamer doesn't know how to move from dream to reality. If you are stopped in your tracks at that point of paralysis, knowing you have the goods to make it, to achieve success, fame, stardom—it's time to take action.

Very few people are simply born with some innate

"it" quality that is unattainable to the rest of us. Trust me. If that's what you believe from watching too many "E! True Hollywood Stories" or reading too many issues of *People* magazine, I am here to tell you that you have been misled. Stars, whether in show business or in any other walk of life, are made, not born.

As a reporter on the nationally renowned *New York Post* "Page Six" gossip column for the past five years, I have seen fame come and go, the famous rise and fall. I have seen how some people know how to work it and some don't, and as a result, I have learned what works and what doesn't and am about to pass on what I've learned to you.

The truth is that with a modicum of talent and a lot of hard work, virtually anyone (guided by some good advice) can move beyond their drab, no-name universe into that cherished inner circle known as the A list.

These rules are valuable not only for those who seek fame, celebrity, and to have their name in lights, but also for anyone who wants to achieve a dream, launch a business, or get their ideal job. If you don't believe me, look at Donald Trump, who in the early nineties, just after proclaiming himself a billionaire for the first time, turned to his then-wife Marla Maples as they passed a bum on the street and said, "That guy has more money than I do." But Donald knows that what he is selling is a dream, a brand—himself! There are thousands upon thousands of examples, on a grander or lesser scale, of individuals who have learned how to harness the techniques of the best PR people (who are, after all, largely responsible for making the famous famous), learned how to use the media, learned how to transform themselves into stars.

So ask yourself: Are you bored with your humdrum life? Have you begun to achieve success in your field, but are at a loss as to how to rise to the very top of it? Are you itching to be fabulous, famous—to be "it"? No worries. Just read on, honey, and think HOT.

## FIND YOUR TALENT, AND OTHER LESSONS MY MOTHER TAUGHT ME

Everyone has a talent, I swear. It may be something esoteric, as in the ability to compose a symphony. On the other hand, it could be something as mundane as being the best housekeeper in town. (Need I remind you of the success of Heloise, Martha Stewart, and the various domestic divas out there, cranking out books and TV shows and making a fortune?) I don't care what your talent is, everyone has something they do well—perhaps even better than anyone else.

So here are the ten rules of talent and getting ahead.

### Rule #1: Find whatever it is you are good at, and do it!

---

*"Pulling a Donald":* When someone makes their own name more famous than their company or their product. Through relentless self-promotion, branding, and other Machiavellian means, they know that they can sell any product off their name. Sort of a "horse before the cart" theory. Well-known perpetrators include Martha Stewart, self-help guru Tony Robbins, and Leona Helmsley.

---

One of the most powerful publicists in New York, who has launched (not to mention saved) the careers of many celebs, including Britney Spears, Sean "Puffy" Combs, and Jennifer Lopez, is Dan Klores. Klores is a congenial man of fifty with salt and pepper hair and beard to match, along with piercing eyes that don't miss a thing. He spent many years living and working down South preparing for the big time before heading home basically to rule New York. I always take his calls.

Over lunch at the sublime DB Bistro Moderne in midtown Manhattan I asked Klores about Donald Trump's reemergence as the poster boy for success. Klores was Trump's publicist for many years. "I've seen Donald Trump build his brand name brilliantly," Klores observed. "His father was just a builder, but Donald always understood the importance of building a brand name and having an ego. The genius is," Klores continued, "what real talent did he have? Well, his talent was how to negotiate, and how to add the new numbers in. He instinctively knew people, he really did."

Along with the gaudy high rises that dot Manhattan's skyline, Trump was so successful at building his own name—mainly through his appearances in the gossip columns and the publication of books like *The Art of the Deal*—that no one really cared that he had no money. He has been so good at maintaining his personal profile that when his bonds went junk, no one blinked an eye. When I was jumping through hoops to get a mortgage for my small house in the Catskills, my mortgage broker, Seth, told me, "Somebody will always lend to him because he is Donald

Trump. His name is worth even more than his buildings." Seth made this observation even before Trump's monster television hit, *The Apprentice*, which is perhaps the best example of brand extension I've ever witnessed.

In other words, Donald Trump was able to identify his own talent (not spend a lot of time on projects that didn't best utilize his skills) and carve out an empire by doing it. Do you want to become the "Donald Trump" of your profession, whether you are a realtor, a baker, an antiques store-owner, or a caterer? Use his career as a road map!

Or take me as an example.

My only real specific talents are writing and being able to talk to a brick in the wall—for hours, if necessary. Within the first thirty minutes I will have gotten that brick's entire life story, have categorized alphabetically its likes and dislikes, and have gleaned the details of its love life (which usually occupies at least another half hour—love is never easy!). But I didn't always know how to translate this "skill," my "gift of gab," into a career.

In all honesty, I would currently be a doctor or lawyer, if not both simultaneously, if my parents had had their way. But during my sophomore year at Emory University in Atlanta, having already completed the majority of my political science major requirements, I had a nervous breakdown of sorts. (Read: I locked myself in my dorm room for over a week, with only the pie-faced pizza delivery boy dropping by at regular intervals to feed me.) During that time, I imagined myself wearing nondescript Jones of New York gray suits for the rest of my life and getting rapists acquitted of their crimes. I began obsessively plucking my leg hairs. I know. It wasn't pretty.

After a week of semi-insanity, I finally worked up the courage to tell my parents that I would not be fulfilling my destiny as they saw it. After making a brief speech about the importance of 401ks, Roth IRAs, and whatnot, they actually accepted my decision, which to them also meant I would end up living at home with them forever. But before my mother could start getting my room ready, I joined the staff of the school newspaper, and knew right away I had found my calling.

I figured out that to be a journalist, one must know how to write (though not always—just ask any editor!), and one must be able to chat up anyone, anytime, and wring their life story out of them without their ever knowing what is happening. Perfect for me, right?

During my career I have written for the women's pages of a national newspaper in England, written lifestyle pieces for men's magazines, gotten a comprehensive financial education from Wall Street traders during my stint as an over-the-counter derivatives reporter (don't ask—I'm still trying to explain it to my mother), and finally, gotten the scoop on the biggest celebrities, the hottest events, or just the juiciest dirt—all because I have a talent for making people comfortable enough to open up to me, and an instinct for what's news. I also had a front-row seat as I watched agents, managers, PR people, stylists, and others create stars.

Had I ultimately decided to go to law school, I'm certain I would have made it through somehow, but I would no doubt have become an absolutely miserable person, and probably not a very good lawyer, slogging away in a back office somewhere, contemplating stabbing myself in the eye with a fork. Which leads me to rule #2.

---

A Raisin: A person who has a dream, but has never gone after it. Instead, they bitterly go about their other business and, like Gollum with the

Ring, obsess, and cradle their dream without ever using it. They are usually the dried-up bitter people who are like the last raisin in the box, smushed up, wrinkly, and, usually, sour. I have always hated raisins.

---

### *Rule #2: Don't try to fake a talent you really don't have!*

You know what I'm talking about. How many times have you seen someone struggling to be something they're not? It may work for a short while, sometimes even for an entire life. But it will never make you happy, and for the most part, people end up spotting you as a fake.

Let's say you want to be a television news anchor, but you can't read a teleprompter no matter how much you practice, you have an awful public-speaking voice, and you don't connect with audiences. Or, like Albert Brooks in *Broadcast News*, you just start sweating buckets as soon as the red light comes on. It's true the first two things can be somewhat overcome via continued practice and voice training, but you will still be left with the fact that you leave your audience cold (and the sweat thing). But say you tried the anchor thing for a while and in the process discovered you have a talent for news writing or for knowing how to recognize a big story. Don't cling to the anchor dream just because that's what you always thought you would be. Adapt, re-think, and become the best damned news producer in the business. Believe me, you will be more satis-fied and more successful.

---

Sometimes you've just got to know when a dream is not attainable. A friend of mine dated a man for many years who was extremely depressed. He had always wanted to be an actor but found him-self as a computer graphics guy instead. When he was younger, he never really went after the dream of acting, assuming something would just fall in his lap. Then later, he did it in a severely half-assed way. Yet he always moaned about wanting to be-come an actor. Because he never got off his ass and did anything in a wholehearted manner, he ended up, at the ripe old age of forty-eight, smok-ing way too much pot, broke, and annoying. Time for another dream, buddy.

---

This syndrome is evident all over, but perhaps nowhere so much as with the "stars" of the reality television shows. After selling themselves (and I do mean selling themselves) on such shows as *The Bachelor*, *The Bachelorette*, *Survivor*, etc., the hapless "winners" always seem to give up their previous professions to try and break into show business, rather than simply accepting that they got lucky once, and going back to what they had before. Zora, the schoolteacher who captured the heart of Evan on the show *Joe Millionaire,* followed up her triumph by getting herself a manager and announcing she would take the sitcom and Home Shopping Network worlds by storm. Sadly, I have yet to see Zora on the tube or any of her "products" she was supposed to be hawking. She got caught up in something that isn't real, isn't authentic, and ditched her true self for a mirage. She should have settled for her fifteen minutes and then returned to planet earth—and her day job.

---

Reality Losers: Those annoying people who go on a reality show and think they should be treated like Meryl Streep. In all facets of life, RLs show up—these people who did a local commercial and think they should be a queen, the entourages of someone semi-famous, the people who don't really *do* anything but through luck or good timing have scored some kind of short-lived attention. To the tune of *The Wizard of Oz* chant "Lions and tigers and bears. Oh my!" repeat after me: "Trista and Ryan and Bob Guiney—yuck!"

---

Speaking of planets, Matthew Rich, whose company is called Planet PR, is a tall, lean, impeccably mannered man who among other things helps the Miss USA pageant groom its winners for entry into public life. He says: "I tell my clients—you have to stay true to yourself. If you don't, it will come through in your presentation."

The media can be ruthless to people who are found to be inauthentic. Steven Gaines is one of the most formidable society journalists out there and has often noted the ability of society to chew people up and spit them out after they are revealed to be something other than they appear. Steven is perhaps the leading expert on Hamptons society and even wrote a book about it, *Philistines at the Hedgerow*. He observes that it is essential, for those who attain fame or notoriety, to "have the goods to back it up." "Tabloid life is very brief," he told me. "It burns bright and hot and then it's over—kind of like those old flashbulbs." If you have faked your way to fame, you're soon going to disappear.

---

A Faux: A fraud, phony, or poser.

---

"Talent" may seem like an intangible quality, but I like to think of it as something practical, a product a person knows how to sell, that has to be cultivated and effectively presented, and that in time will become something the public will clamor for. R. Couri Hay, a fixture in New York society and someone who has helped pave the way for the most prominent queen bees to take their places at the top of the social pecking order, advises, "You've got to have something to sell. You're a dermatologist, you're a decorator, you're a designer." He offers a warning, one that may seem obvious, but one which all too many people ignore: "If you're no good, people are going to know it. It's very hard to fake it for long."

*Rule #3: Don't know what you're good at?*
*Ask someone to help you figure it out.*

This is tricky. What if you really have no idea what you're good at? Maybe you just haven't had the right sort of feedback or mentoring, you always went along with your father's desire that you become an engineer, but one day you woke up and realized you just can't do it anymore. Problem is, you've never spent any time figuring out what you *do* want to do, what your real talent is.

Gary Greenberg, a successful comic and author of *Be Prepared,* told me about what a pal of his (let's call him Jim) decided to do when he came to this crossroads. Jim was in banking, and on paper was doing well enough. But he was deeply unhappy, and the truth was, it showed in all sorts of ways. He performed all of his job responsibilities competently, but none particularly well. However, he had no idea how to make a change, or what he wanted to change into.

Then Jim had a brainstorm. He decided to send out a questionnaire to his closest friends and family members.

A Sample Questionnaire:

- What are my best qualities?
- What are my worst?
- Are there some things I do better than anyone else?
- Besides karaoke, are there some things I think I am good at, but really not? [Unless you want to be a singer, then take out the karaoke bit]
- What can I do that no one else can do?
- When you need help from me, what do you call me for?
- If you could pick out the perfect (legal, please) career for me, what would it be and why?
- When have you seen me happiest, career-wise?

Jim knew he needed some perspective and some objectivity, and he decided to rely on those closest to him to help.

He was astounded by the similarity of the responses. Nearly all of his friends wrote back that they thought he was especially good at event planning.

23

They said he was extremely good at picking the right people for the right places, at putting compatible groups of friends together. All felt that he intuitively knew the best, most appropriate venues for parties and other special occasions.

After mulling over the results for a brief time, Jim left banking and used his savings to start an events company. Today he runs one of the most lucrative events and catering companies in New Jersey, and is successful beyond his wildest dreams. He is also happy. So remember, sometimes the people closest to us know us better than we know ourselves!

### Rule #4: Learn to enjoy the spotlight: Be the star of your own stage.

Not everyone likes being the center of attention. Some people would rather sit back and watch what's going on around them than participate. Unlike you, who, if you are reading this book, probably enjoy the limelight or want to learn how, they don't like it when all eyes in the room turn their way. But if what you really want is to climb the ladder, get to the top, see your name in lights, and you haven't yet gotten off your duff, are pretending to be modest, or are just shy, to those people I say the following: GET OVER IT. I don't care how you do it. Get a therapist.

Practice speaking in front of a mirror or in front of your pals. But one way or another, get over it.

There is an old maxim whose basic message is that it is better to say little or nothing than to say a lot. I violently disagree with this. I think wallflowers are dull.

---

Verbal Vomit vs. Conversation: There is a difference. We have all been seated next to that certain someone at dinner parties, on airplanes, whatnot. You know, that person who doesn't SHUT UP. Someone who, thirty minutes into their monologue, they have told you about the first thirty minutes of their day . . . and you want to strangle them. There is a difference between someone who has something to add to the conversation and the person who simply likes to hear their own voice. When I say "Don't be a wallflower," I mean ADD to the conversation, don't monopolize it. A good conversation starts with a good listener and ends with someone who can make a point concisely and knowledgeably. I have a friend, we'll call her Susie. She is a lovely, amazing human being. Sadly, her voice can cut glass and with every cocktail, the decibels reach yet another eardrum-popping level. No matter how many times people "shush" her or say, "Susie, keep it down"—or worse, try to get a sentence in—she just keeps barging ahead like a train out of control. DON'T become a Susie.

---

One of the things I have learned in my years of being a gossip columnist is that you don't necessarily need to be the smartest person in the room, or the most talented, in order to get ahead. Being a loudmouth can really help. I've noticed that when people say things loudly and strongly—confidently enough (and have the information to back it up)—people will listen. When it counts, try to command the room's attention, have faith in what you say, and say it with confidence. Use eye contact, a few well-chosen words, and your physical presence: how you dress, how you carry yourself. If *you* don't believe in yourself, who will?

---

Even dinner parties are work. And by *work*, I don't mean the labor involved in throwing the party. If you are invited to a dinner party, you should come prepared to join in the conversation, to really contribute something to it—to sing for your supper. Being an entertaining guest will guarantee that you will be invited back, that the investor you met at the table will remember you and want to help finance the company you are starting or hire you to be the company's spokesperson. Look at every social occasion as an opportunity, because it is!

---

When I first started at Page Six in the fall of 1999, one of the first parties I attended was for the premiere of the film *Any Given Sunday*, starring Samuel L. Jackson. All sorts of Hollywood stars and agents were there, along with the movie's producers and directors. Everyone there was someone, but one corner of the room seemed to be generating the loudest, most excited buzz. I admit that I was one of those who gathered around to see who it was who was enjoying the limelight. I saw a petite, bleached blonde busily getting her picture taken and just eating up the attention. Who was it? Lizzie Grubman, who at the time was "just" a publicist (this was obviously before her infamous car accident in Southampton which would propel her to global notoriety or her new show *Power Girls* on MTV). But even back then she had a certain star quality, which was really just a belief in herself and her own fabulousness. She knew what to say and when to say it, and she said it just loudly enough so that everyone paid attention. And wow, did she know how to work the PR thing. Which brings me to Rule #5.

### Rule #5: Educate yourself. Knowledge is power.

Lizzie Grubman is not the best educated, most book-smart person in the universe. She dropped out of Boston University during her sophomore year to start promoting local nightclubs. Later, she moved back to New York, where her family is from, to work for a variety of public relations firms before starting her own company, Lizzie Grubman P.R. She has represented such individuals as Jay-Z, Damon Dash, and Jeff Kwatinetz, as well as companies such as Puma, Sony, and Roc-A-Fella Records. "I am not a book person," she freely admits, confessing to reading only Danielle Steele novels as far as literature is concerned. On the other hand, she devours four newspapers every single morning, and is up to date on all manner of current events, especially those involving the social world and Hollywood—information that is crucial to her PR business.

Lizzie is also an expert on her own industry, tracking and monitoring the world of public relations—

she knows what everyone is doing and where they're doing it.

In the fall of 2002, when she uttered the words: "PR is dead; marketing is where it's at," everyone took notice. Love her or hate her, Lizzie always knows what she is talking about, and she was right—everything today is about branding and building a franchise.

---

Must-reads:

- *The New York Times*
- The *New York Post*, in particular, Page Six (www.nypost.com)
- *The Wall Street Journal* (if in business)
- Your local paper—preferably the main paper and the alternative weekly
- The *Drudge Report* (www.drudgereport. com), a great compilation of breaking news
- One newsweekly, be it *Time*, *Newsweek,* or *The Economist*
- At *least* one celebrity weekly, either *US Weekly*, *People*, *Star*, the *National Enquirer,* or *In Touch*. Even if you are not interested in celebrities, these magazines offer great in-

sight into marketing people, products, and knowing what's hot.

- Of the monthlies: For more bang for your buck, pick magazines that offer guidance, such as *Marie Claire*, *Glamour*, *Cosmopolitan*, *Lucky*, or *Cargo*. For reading pleasure, try *Vogue*, *Elle*, or *Vanity Fair*.
- www.Foxnews.com
- www.Cnn.com
- www.Gawker.com. This is a fabulously funny New York site which has an ironic take on most everything, while keeping you informed. Its sister sites, wonkette.com (a Washington D.C.–based site) and Defamer.com (Los Angeles) are also excellent. Even if you don't live in these cities, you should think cosmopolitan and know what's going on!
- www.msnbc.com's gossip columnist Jeannette Walls

You know what I'm getting at. Whatever your field is, become the world's leading expert in it. Education in that area is your crucial hobby. This may mean going to night school, taking a class, or simply regularly reading certain trade periodicals or newspapers. Being knowledgeable in your field enables you to go anywhere and speak with confidence.

### *Rule #6: Formulate a flexible plan of attack, and stick to it.*

So what do you do if you are not exactly where you want to be? Make a list. Make a plan. It doesn't have to be an instant thing. Make it a four-year plan—even a ten-year plan. Just be sure it feels reasonable and that you can stick to it—and then, stick to it!! Think of the plan as your committed partner, and realize that if the plan is going to work for you, you must also work for the plan. Remember that every step you take after laying out your plan is a step in the right direction—even though it may be only one step. View every job you do, every chore you take on, as a valuable and important component of the plan.

Let me give you an example. Let's say you want to become the head copywriter at an advertising firm, but the only position available that you are currently qualified for is secretary for an advertising firm. Go for that job. Know that every memo you type for your boss reflects on your overall abilities. Talk to everyone, learn from things going on around you, volunteer for overtime or ask to do extra work in your field of choice. Nothing should be done halfway or with a bad attitude. Every company is always looking for its own success stories, looking to promote from within. People are always hoping to find team players who take initiative and who cover their jobs competently and cheerfully. "Luck" has very little to do with getting ahead. You can make your own luck!

Jillian Kogan is a producer for MTV in Los Angeles, and has seen dozens of wannabe musicians ascend from performing in the street to filling 60,000-seat arenas. She confirms that commitment and dedication are key to those successes. She says that "tenacity and having a whole bunch of want-to, as an old Texas football coach friend of mine always says, is important as well."

---

QVC Hacks: Many well-known people have hawked their wares on the Home Shopping Network, QVC, and other cable outlets, making them millionaires. Kathy Hilton, Rocco DiSpirito, Star Jones, Suzanne Somers, furrier Dennis Basso, and Bob Mackie, among others, have turned themselves into household names and bulked up their bank accounts by shilling their wares on cable.

---

I love the example of fashion designer Randolph Duke.

Twenty years ago, Randolph was a struggling nobody. But he'd always dreamed of becoming a designer and making a (good) living out of it. He was good at networking, made some connections, and began to create beautiful gowns. He appeared to be well on his way to becoming a top couturier, which is unfortunately where his problems started. Matthew Rich, who handles PR for Duke, told me that as good as Randolph was at making gorgeous couture dresses, it was "costing him $22,000 to make a $20,000 dress." This is where having a plan, and staying focused on it, even when things don't unfold as you'd anticipated, is key. As Matthew put it, "Sometimes what you really, really love to do, and are very good at, won't make you money." In Randolph Duke's case, he almost went out of business. But instead of packing up his dream and going down in defeat, he did something he never imagined he could or would do: He started selling an inexpensive line of clothing on QVC, giving up expensive couture for cheaper, mass-merchandised material. "Sometimes you have to do other things to sustain you so you can also do the things you love," Rich observed.

Thanks to a vision and a long-term view, Randolph Duke is now back in the black and making money hand over fist doing what he loved to do best—that is, designing clothes.

I hate clichés, but in this case the old saying "patience is a virtue" really sums it up (and this is coming from someone who freaks out when she is five minutes late or has to wait ten minutes for a meal in a restaurant). When I say that your plan can be long-term, I mean it. Nothing good happens right away. Even if it did, chances are you wouldn't be ready to handle it. Plans help to initiate a process, and success requires that a certain process occur, which gives you the chance to develop perspective.

When I worked for the British newspaper *The Guardian*, from 1995 to 1997, I learned an extremely valuable lesson in patience and experience from my boss, Clare Longrigg, who was then editor of the women's pages. I told Clare how frustrated I was that my career as a journalist wasn't taking off fast enough, and that I was thinking about quitting to enroll in the prestigious Columbia School of Journalism, which not only would have meant giving up my job but also incurring $40,000 or so in debt. I felt like maybe I needed that piece of paper, not to mention the contacts I would acquire by attending the school. I don't know if I expected a pat on the head or what, but her response was not what I'd anticipated. She looked at me sharply and declared, "Paula, it's not like journalism is brain surgery, which would require massive amounts of studying. It is a craft that needs to be learned by doing. Just do it and you will build yourself up and be successful by DOING it." She was right. All these years later I think of Clare and silently thank her. Because now I know that if by some act of fate British *Vogue* had called that day and offered me a job, I would have taken it—and have been fired almost immediately. I wasn't yet ready for that level of job. Instead, I slogged my way through various journalism jobs, all the while taking on side jobs to pay the rent, and I learned my craft bit by bit. I'm glad I didn't peak too soon. A career takes time to mature and develop, just as a person does. Clare saved me $45,000 (one year's tuition at Columbia grad school) and steeled my resolve to keep working away at my dream instead of taking a costly detour.

---

Pulling a Brady: Named after the Brady Bunch kids, it's when someone peaks too early. Some of the drawbacks of peaking too early can be, no one will ever see you as anything but your early famous incarnation; there's nowhere to go from the top but down; and if you have tasted success early and easily, you never learn the lessons that come from hard work and poverty.

---

If you don't believe me, think about the legions of child actors who become stars too early and then can't deal with their fame, money, and good fortune. They end up crashing and burning. Need I say Corey Feldman or, God forbid, Dana Plato? No one should have to be embarrassed by their *E! True Hollywood Story* or *A&E Biography*!

---

An Al Bundy: Named after the *Married . . . with Children* character, this is the guy who was once a Brady and can't get over the fact that his fifteen minutes of fame has come and gone. He will obsessively bore you with detailed stories of his exploits in "the good old days" and never be able to move on.

---

Work toward your goal. Don't be afraid to stumble, but always get back up and dust yourself off. Don't forget the game plan, and above all, be patient. You will become unstoppable!

***Rule #7: If you want it enough, you can get it—but don't sell yourself short.***

When you want something badly, sometimes you get desperate. An offer comes your way and it's not quite what you want, but you take it anyway, because you're afraid that the thing you really want will never happen. That is called settling for second best, and it is a big mistake.

Julie Greenwald, a self-described "Jewish girl from the Catskills" who is now an executive at Warner Music, offered this advice in *Elle* magazine: "Never speak cryptically. Be straight with people. If you try to be too clever and roundabout, people will miss what you are saying. And communicate not just by the way you speak but with body language, by looking someone dead in the eye."

(Note: this is not a good thing to do while driving. Just ask my mother, who gets creeped out if she is talking to someone and they don't look her in the eye. Hence, four cars totaled in under two years.)

The bottom line is, the worst that can happen is that the answer will be no—and then you can move on and get what you need elsewhere, or at least negotiate for the best consolation prize you can get!

Julie Greenwald did admit in *Elle* that she had told a white lie or two to get in the door of Island Def Jam's CEO Lyor Cohen's office. She said: "The first day I met Lyor I walked in and he says, 'Why should I hire you?' and I say, 'Because I'm smart, because I am a fast learner, and because I can type fifty-five words a minute.'" She was hired. About two months later, however, he noticed Julie couldn't type. He asked her why she lied. Her answer? "Dude—who cares now? I'm a great assistant!"

Despite her tiny little dishonesty, in the end she had the goods to back it up. And while I'm not recommending that you lie to get in the door (no doubt about it—this can backfire), Julie knew what she wanted, knew she could do the job, and she got it.

### Rule #8: Never be mean to waiters—what goes around comes around.

When I was a teenager and just beginning to date, my mother gave me a few choice pieces of advice. The first was "Never date a man with a van." What can I tell you?

She's a neurotic Jewish woman from Queens. In Queens, a van always meant stolen goods or rapists inside. In Ohio, where I grew up, it also meant sex in the back.

The second rule, even more important, was "Always notice how your date treats your waiter, because in the end, that's how he will treat you." I have used this rule over and over again in my life. The older I get, the more I realize it's a small world, and those you treat badly will come back to bite you!

It is well known in the gossip "community" that if you want to get some piece of information out there but don't want it to be traced back to you—as that would be considered crass—simply tell ten people you know who can't keep a secret (you know who you are). Those ten will tell another ten, and so on. Pretty soon, everyone will know everything. The point is, very few people can keep their mouths shut. Now, what if something annoying happened and you lost your temper and started screaming and carrying on? If just one person who can't keep his mouth shut sees you, the next day, everyone will know about it, whether you like it or not.

Always watch what you say. In the end, inevitably,

you will be judged by your own words and actions. I also like to think of it this way: today's assistant could end up being tomorrow's boss!

Take Dina Wise, director of Special Events for Miramax Films, and my pal. She once had an assistant named Nicky Landow. Dina took Nicky under her wing, became her mentor. Nicky later moved to Los Angeles and got a great job in development for Fox. No matter what, Dina knows if she ever needs anything from Nicky, Nicky would do it instantly.

Or take my boss, Richard Johnson. He wields a lot of power, and perhaps a lesser man wouldn't have wielded it so kindly. Richard has always mentored the people who work for him. He recognizes that if he trains someone well, even if they end up leaving to work somewhere else, if they look good, so will he. And trust me, there is nothing like being trained by or having worked with Richard Johnson to give you instant credibility in New York. You would be hard-pressed to find anyone who has a bad word to say about Richard. People trust him, and so he gets great stories. By being a gentleman and having good manners, Richard has ended up increasing his power tenfold.

Waiter, there's a fly in my soup: Unpleasant things
happen. Put them in perspective. A big blowup,
feud, or fight is not going to make things better.
Get rid of the nasty fly ASAP and resume your
meal as if nothing ever happened.

Couri Hay, who has witnessed a lot of rises and
falls, quotes the old adage, Be nice to people on the
way up, because you never know when you're going
to need them on the way down.

A less well known example of this phenomenon is
Peggy Siegal, who in the nineties was one of the
most powerful PR people in the movie business. She
single-handedly got to decide who would and
wouldn't walk the red carpet, and she spent most of
her time currying favor with the rich and powerful.
She lived in New York but had a lot of clout in L.A.
too. Her Rolodex was filled with the biggest names
in the business. There wasn't anyone she couldn't
get on the phone. But she made a fatal mistake in
that she was never very nice to her underlings, people she deemed not useful, or anyone she arbitrar-
ily decided didn't matter. Unfortunately, Peggy was

rude to one too many people who really *did* matter, despite her lack of recognition. We wrote this about Peggy in September 2004:

## PUBLICIST FEELS STUDIO'S WRATH

POWER publicist Peggy Siegal may have ousted the wrong man from his seat at the movie premiere for "Mean Girls" earlier this year.

Sources say the fearless flak didn't recognize Gerry Rich, president of Paramount's worldwide marketing, and demanded that he give up his seat to someone Siegal deemed more important.

Now Siegal, who specializes in hosting A-list screenings crammed with socialites and bold-faced names, is in a panic because the suits at Paramount have iced her in the wake of her mis-guided move.

"It sparked a big brouhaha, and now the studio's refused to work with her again," a source told PAGE SIX.

"Peggy is, literally, freaking out. It's really bad. She's completely unglued over it."

Spies said Siegal—who began her career as an assistant to the legendary public-relations genius Bobby Zarem—has launched a full-on groveling campaign, in which she's inundated Rich and others at Paramount with calls, begging for mercy.

Siegal's even resorted to bribery—having bottles of Veuve Clicquot champagne and Belvedere vodka delivered to Paramount heavyweights.

"Apparently, her reputation in New York is being challenged, and she is desperate to save face," said an insider.

A Paramount spokesman said the studio would have no comment. But an insider confirmed there was bad blood between Siegal and Paramount that went beyond Gerry Rich.

The blacklisting comes at a particularly bad time for Siegal, who had hoped to use her Paramount connection to arrange a charity event for the venerable Princess Grace Foundation, sources said.

Siegal pitched the possibility of the Foundation hosting the premiere of Paramount's upcoming "SpongeBob SquarePants" movie—a big screen version of the wildly popular Nickelodeon cartoon.

"Paramount has to give permission but they're digging in their heels, refusing to deal with Peggy," snarked a spy. Siegal did not return calls from PAGE SIX.

Today, her business is a shadow of what it once was in its heyday. Karma is a bitch, and in the end, she will always come to collect from you.

***Rule #9: People are going to hate you, so have a hide like a rhino—and above all, don't give them a reason to bring you down!***

Let me just get this out of the way: if you do drugs, drink to excess, or are addicted to anything that's not good for you, STOP. NOW. And cut out of your life like a cancer people who drink to excess, do drugs, gamble, or do other detrimental things.

Take the sad story of Maggie Rizer as an example. She was once one of the top supermodels, earning millions. She made the mistake of entrusting her finances to her stepfather, a chronic gambler who bet away her fortune. In 2002, she found out she was totally broke, which meant that instead of resting on her laurels, she had to get back out there at precisely the time a model's career is just about over.

To be successful, you have to look over your shoulder a little bit and stay away from the things and people that are going to bring you down. And keep an eye on where you came from, but don't let that define or rule you either.

I remember talking to Russell Simmons several years ago during Sean "Puffy" Combs's trial for gun possession. Puffy had been in a nightclub with his then girlfriend J.Lo and a protégé called Shine. There had been a fight. There were gunshots.

Russell, the founder of Def Jam and billionaire owner of Phat Farm and other companies, observed that he too, like Puffy, grew up in the ghetto, but had worked long and hard to get out. He told me, "I don't need to prove my street cred by hanging out with thugs. I have moved on."

If something in your life threatens to tarnish or even ruin you, don't be afraid to cut it loose and move on.

Howard Karren used to be an editor at *New York* magazine and now works at the magazine *Premiere*. He has witnessed the rise and fall of a celebrity or two, and says this about fame: "There is a price to pay. If you are 'It,' other people aren't, and that means they are going to be angry. You have to be secure in your own sense of accomplishment, because other people are going to hate you for it. You gotta be able to defend that, to put up certain walls, borders. I've seen young actors and actresses starting off in the media, that tend to be honest in the beginning. They learn to lie. They learn to say nothing about things they don't want to talk about, and to find something entertaining to distract people from topics they want to avoid. They learn to encapsulate their feelings in very simple ways that are clearly expressed. All these things happen over time."

### Rule #10: If you aren't going to do something— stop bitching and stay home.

Woody Allen once said, "Ninety-nine percent of success is just showing up."

Sometimes the hardest thing is taking the first step.

I was often miserable in college. I wanted to take a year off. Go to Europe. Do anything other than what I was doing. But I stayed in college, and I'm glad I did. Still, once I graduated, I was stuck. What was next? I still wanted to go to Europe, but I was anxiety ridden. My parents weren't wealthy and college had been expensive. The most practical thing was to stay home and work. Even when some friends decided to go to London and asked me to come, I hesitated. I was paralyzed with fear. But I decided to go, and you know what? It was easy! Within a month I had scored a job at *The Guardian*. And the only thing that made me mad was how easy it had ended up being, and the realization that I almost hadn't gone because some people had told me I couldn't or shouldn't. I had almost not gone out of fear.

To me, "I can't" is the most annoying phrase in the English language. Not only *can* you but you *will*— you must! If anyone tells you you can't, drop them like a hot potato. There is no room in anyone's life for naysayers.

So get out there already!

## Chapter Two

# Attitude + Dedication = SUCCESS

T HERE IS A COMMON MISCONCEPTION THAT PEOPLE who make it to the top—whether they are movie stars breaking box-office records, fashion designers winning awards and building financial empires, or the owner of the local wine shop who has been successful enough to contemplate opening a second store—got where they are through dumb luck, nepotism, or some other advantage that got them what hard work alone never could. While I can't say there is absolutely no truth in that perspective— witness Tori Spelling—for the most part, it has been my experience that true and lasting success is attained mainly by having a good, positive attitude, being completely committed to a clear goal, and dedicating yourself to realizing that dream.

In my profession, I look to people like those divine divas Liz Smith and Cindy Adams, who work long, hard hours and are never too proud or too high and mighty to roll up their sleeves and work the story or the stars on the red carpet at a premiere. I also idolize Katharine Graham, the late publisher of the *Washington Post*. Talk about attitude, commitment, and dedication! She had a husband who was unfaithful, mentally unstable, and occupied a position as head of the *Post*, a position that was really rightfully hers. Nevertheless, she was an excellent wife and mother, but when her husband died, she stepped up to the plate and did what no one thought she could: She ran the *Washington Post* and helped make it into one of the greatest newspapers of our time. Yes, her family owned the paper. But instead of resting on her laurels or being the spoiled rich girl, she started at the bottom, learned the newspaper business, and was always the hardest working person in the room.

---

Worker bees: The people who will stay up from dawn till dusk making sure they get their—and sometimes others'—work done. Everything is an opportunity and there is no task too insurmountable. If they—or you—need something done they will find a way to do it, even if initially, they don't know how. My friend Dina Wise, whom I quote in this book, is the perfect example. She is the perfect employee. She is the party planner for Miramax Films—and every party she does comes off without a hitch. In addition, if her boss needs her to pinch hit in another area, she will—without complaining. Dina may be an employee today but in a near tomorrow she will run a company, and well, with all the skills, tenacity, and daring she uses now.

Or look at Paris Hilton, someone who could have just been a snotty little heiress and nothing else. Your own personal goals may not resemble Paris Hilton's in any way, but you've got to admit that by working her "platform," tirelessly cultivating an image as a hard-partying, globe-trotting fashionista, she has attained a certain kind of iconic success.

To become a name, you've got to make sure people know what your name is, but you've also got to develop the internal mindset of confidence and persistence that will enable you to keep your eyes on the prize. The most successful people I write about as a Page Six columnist, the most successful people I know, are always professional when they need to be. They dedicate themselves to schmoozing, cultivating, cajoling—and to delivering. If you've already reached the Tom Cruise/Tom Hanks levels of fame and success, chances are you are not reading this book. But those two gentlemen are good examples of what I'm talking about. They do not rely on their reputations to keep them on top.

In the case of Hanks, not only does he choose great material and deliver it beautifully, but everyone who has worked with him says that he is as hard working and professional as anyone they've ever met, that he doesn't throw star tantrums, that he is unfailingly courteous and friendly. Tom Cruise, by all reports, is a perfectionist who does not rest until he gets it right, and who, though he no longer has any real need to cultivate additional press, is always professional, punctual, and courteous when duty calls.

---

The three P's to live by: Professionalism, Punctuality, and Personality. Practice all three, or you will stall just out of the starting gate. And always keep in mind: Tantrums are for babies. If there's an issue, figure out a calm, collected way to work it out. You will win more admirers for having a calm demeanor than for losing your head.

There are countless showbiz examples of what I'm talking about in terms of behind-the-scenes talent as well. Most people I know agree that Rick Yorn is an excellent example of someone who has found his calling and does his job brilliantly. He is a manager whose clients include Leonardo DiCaprio and Cameron Diaz and other huge stars. According to Jillian Kogan, people seem to flock to him not so much because of what he is saying as because "there's a chemistry that he puts off . . . not being threatened, a little bit of fearlessness. I think there are people who come off very quickly as phonies, and people who come off as being genuine." Yorn and, according to Kogan, Ron Meyer, a founder of CAA, are two people who have developed big personalities that work for them.

This is a plus in any field, whether you are running your local real estate office, managing the town's bank, launching a wine bar, or selling encyclopedias door to door.

Let's say you own a successful restaurant, but want to open another. Hopefully, you will have installed a good management system at your first restaurant so that you can open the other. But in opening the new restaurant you will have to work as if it is your first, sometimes pitching in as a busboy, waiter, host, or manager if need be. As we all know, new businesses always have kinks. Simply resting on the laurels of your first restaurant and expecting people to flock to your new one because of your name is not acceptable. The second restaurant has to be just as good, just as efficient, and just as clean. Rocco DiSpirito learned that rule (and we all watched as he learned it) on NBC's *The Restaurant.*

Rocco was already the chef and proprietor of a three-star Manhattan restaurant, Union Pacific, when he teamed up with Jeffrey Chodorow to open his namesake eatery, Rocco's. But in doing so, Rocco became enamored of himself, and spent more time promoting his books, his visage, and his brand name than actually cooking in the kitchen. When the reviews came out, they were scathing. The *New York Post* gave Rocco's no stars and noted that it might have given it one star—*maybe*—if Rocco's other restaurant, Union Pacific, wasn't so good. Sadly, due to Rocco's lack of attention, Union Pacific also suffered and was cut down to two stars later that year and the owners of Union Pacific booted Rocco for another chef who had more time to devote to the actual kitchen. So, take note. Every new project is worth doing and worth spending all of your time and commitment on. It is exhausting, but you got yourself into it. It's like giving birth to another child.

Uber-publicist Desiree Gruber, who co-owns the publicity firm Full Picture, has a well-developed nose for recognizing new talent. She represents big stars like supermodel Heidi Klum and Arnold Schwarzenegger (in his acting capacity, *not* as governor of California), among countless others. What does she look for when she considers taking on someone new? She told me that when taking on a new client, whether an individual or a corporation (she also represents such companies as Victoria's Secret and Kmart), that it's important to "genuinely believe in the client—in their sensibility, talent, philosophy, and objectives—to be genuinely excited about promoting the client and having a mutual respect. On a practical level, a client has to bring a certain level of prestige and/or financial compensation, but also the client has to be receptive to putting themselves out there in the right ways. Helping an entertainer doesn't work unless they have their own drive, their own desire to excel, and to bring the best of themselves to the table." She says, "A home run is when you connect with talent who really loves what they do and wants to put in the hours to get the message out," whether it's going to events, responding to requests, "playing the game" a little. "With young aspiring talent, whether in music, film, fashion, or politics, it's a numbers game. The more people you put them in front of who can connect with and believe in them, the more opportunities arise."

I asked Desiree to give me an example of someone who has achieved success by using this formula, and she cited Heidi Klum. Obviously, the beautiful Heidi has the goods to back it up, but "she was able to jump off the pages of *Sports Illustrated* and the Victoria's Secret catalogue by helping the consumer get to know her personally via the media. When presented with the daunting task of facing the media after getting her first *SI* cover, she took the time to make each journalist feel like she was answering the questions for the first time. She even remembered the names of each of the writers, which communicated to them that she respected them. That's the kind of commitment and professionalism I look for in my clients."

When I asked Dan Klores for examples of someone who has made it primarily through grit and drive, Sean Combs was the first name that came to him. He told me, "That guy works twenty hours a day." Sure he wanted to break out of the pack and become famous, but he was never the prima donna about it. Klores recalls, "He was an assistant and a club promoter. A nobody. In business circles, that guy is referred to as an earner. And he had a vision."

---

You can sleep when you are dead: Especially when starting out, you must be disciplined and understand that sleep is a luxury. There is a lot to do in a small amount of time, and the more you put off for tomorrow the less chance you will have for success. In addition to building your brand, image, company, and wardrobe, there are other things to consider. Take my pal Amy Sacco. Amy owns the two hottest clubs in New York, Bungalow 8 and Lot 61. In addition to manning her clubs every night, she also goes to two or three social events or cocktail parties a night because she knows that when she sees people out, she is not only a walking billboard for her clubs, but she can also wrangle everyone back to her places to spend their hard-earned cash.

---

Klores also sees Arianna Huffington as someone who has completely thrown herself into the act of self-creation, or in her case, re-creation. Years ago she was known as a sort of party girl who had had a lot of "lovers," or "lov-uhs," as Sarah Jessica Parker so famously called them in one of the last episodes of *Sex and the City*. She married a very wealthy guy and was seen as the ambition and brains behind his quest for a senate seat. He lost, they divorced, and then what was she going to do? People had begun to perceive her as the sort of demon queen behind the right wing throne, and when that didn't pan out, she had to come up with something new. So, according to Klores, "She hires a Hollywood manager and they come up with a strategy, a real strategy. Take it slow. Take it easy, but the first thing we'll do is get you a syndicated news column. Twenty, thirty, fifty papers buy it. Then we have to lighten your image. This was my doing. I had her do an ad campaign for Comedy Central. This right-wing woman with Al Franken, in bed. I represented Comedy Central, and I represented her. So that's how she started moving along."

When I ask people about drive and who has it, inevitably people mention Jennifer Lopez. In my opinion, Jennifer Lopez is a mediocre singer, and she certainly isn't a great actress. Sure, guys think she's hot, but she's not the biggest natural beauty out there. So what has gotten her to where she is? Rachel Felder, who spent many years working at Columbia Records and *People* magazine and is now a freelance writer, says that Lopez rarely stops working, that sometimes she will be simultaneously shooting a movie and recording a record, and so she'll shoot all day and then record until four in the morning. Felder said that from the time she was a kid, Lopez "always told everyone she was going to be famous, and she seems always to have had that conviction and drive."

---

One man's trash is another man's treasure, but document everything! Always have more than one idea on hand, but make sure everyone knows your ideas are your own, and not easily usurped by someone else. Write them down, e-mail them to yourself, I don't care, just document! My pal Bradly, before he became a big-time television producer for *Entertainment Tonight*, worked for another show. One day his boss asked him for several ideas for guests to book on the talk show. Bradly shot out ten or twelve people right off the bat, and instead of praising him, his boss sneered: "God, those ideas suck! They are just awful, leave me be!" and kicked him out of her office and shut her door. Three minutes later, eager beaver Bradly had more ideas, walked into his boss's office and found her on the phone with the show's executive producer, telling him all of Bradly's ideas as if they were her own. The point is, always be professional and eager, but make sure you have your butt covered too. Your co-worker may seem really fab, but who really knows anyone unless they have fought for you in battle?

━━━━━━━━━━━━━━━━━━━━━━━━━━━

When I think of people who have both a firm belief in their own fabulousness and the sort of dogged determination we're talking about, someone I admire for her commitment and dedication, who has used her own quirks, interests, and talents to become a huge radio success, I think of NPR's *Fresh Air* host Terry Gross. Terry's show is considered one that can catapult a book to bestsellerdom, or make a record a hit. In real life, she is a tiny, fragile-looking woman with large glasses and a voice like a little girl's, even though she is in her late forties or fifties. She is a little bit shy, and not at all forceful-seeming. But on the air, she is commanding and fearless, and her voice is resonant. I know she has worked to make that voice fuller and stronger, and that she has probably also worked hard to learn to ask the sorts of probing questions she does. But what most impresses me about her is that invariably it's clear that she is prepared. She does her homework. If she's interviewing a musician, she knows everything there is to know about her work, past and present. A writer can count on the fact that she's read his book just out, and all his previous ones too. That's why she gets the best guests, and that's why people like Sean Penn, who famously dislikes being interviewed, don't seem to mind being interviewed by her. She *has* made herself an indispensable media personality, and published her own book, *All I Did Was Ask*.

I have tried to follow these rules on my own job. On a typical day at my desk at the *New York Post*, or when doing television broadcasts for *Entertainment Tonight*, I am hard at work following a story from start to finish. Often I have been out late the night before, attending a film opening, a magazine launch, an HBO party. I know that probably doesn't sound like hard work, but it is an essential part of my job, and it's exhausting. I have just been at the office all day. I have just enough time to dash home, perhaps take a shower, throw on some clothes and makeup, and go out in search, hopefully, of tomorrow's big scoop. By the time I get home it is frequently after midnight, and sleep doesn't come easily, despite how tired I am. The next morning it's up early and off to the *Post* again, where the phones will ring ceaselessly, and the never-ending search for good items will continue. What keeps me going? I like to think about what got me here from Ohio. Did I imagine that my name would be on a nationally known column, or that I would be appearing regularly on a national TV show? For that matter, did I think Miramax Books would give me a book contract? Of course not. I did have some inkling that I was ambitious, that I didn't want to work in an insurance office, and as I've already mentioned, I really didn't want to become a lawyer. I don't mind working seven days a week, however many hours a day, because I love what I do, and I think that too is what distinguishes all of the successful people I'm talking about—they love what they do.

Learn how to multitask. Now, it's ironic for me to be telling you since . . . well, I have trouble driving a car and smoking a cigarette at the same time . . . but in other areas of my life, I can juggle just fine. Because building the brand that is you takes many skills and involves doing several different things at once, you will have to learn how to multitask. A helpful hint: Write everything down in a diary. Make schedules and stick to them. Plan out the day and the week ahead. Anything to keep your eye on the ball.

---

Not too long ago, I saw David Remnick, editor of *The New Yorker*, give a talk at a big journalistic event. I happen to know, through people who work at *The New Yorker*, that David is a very hands-on editor who reads everything in his weekly magazine, has a lot to say about its content and style, and also finds time to write quite a bit himself. And yet there he was, speaking passionately about what is going on in Russia today, and how journalists there are experiencing more and more censorship. The first book he wrote was about Russia, and he is a leading expert on that part of the world. With all of the responsibility he now has for running one of the most important magazines in the country, where does he find the time not only to keep up on what's happening on such an important foreign-affairs issue, but to write and present such an eloquent and impassioned speech? The point is, this is a passion with David—and he always makes time for his passion. To him, extra work is not a chore, but rather, another great thing to be done well.

To me, that's what gets to the heart of what it means to want success, to be successful, to be a star. Most people who reach the top of their fields, whether they're David Remnick or Madonna or the owner of a bakery, are genuinely inspired and passionate about their work. For them, what they do is not tedious, not just a job to be done and gotten through. In the case of Madonna, it means she goes out there every few years with a new look, a new sound, a new tour theme; similar rules apply if you're the guy in a small Ohio town launching your own accounting firm. You need to know your stuff, know how to get people to pay attention to you, believe in your own worth and fabulousness, and dedicate yourself to going out there and doing it.

---

Chutzpah: A Yiddish word my grandma used to use all the time (especially when I'd ask her for "grandma graft," or money) which means an inordinate amount of gall, brass, or nerve. Everyone needs a little bit of chutzpah if they are going to get anywhere. Remember, success is not for the meek!

It's probably easy to assume that the biggest and most powerful among us are exempt from these rules, but they're not. Leslee Dart is a former partner in the super-powered PR firm PMK, who handled publicity for Nicole Kidman, Tom Hanks, and Hugh Grant, to name a few. She told me that, among other things, what really makes a superstar stand out from the pack is the level of commitment, dedication, and willingness to go that extra mile, even though they're "big stars" and perhaps could get away with less. She told me a story about a time she went to the Venice Film Festival with Nicole Kidman, who arrived in Venice only about an hour before they were scheduled to appear on the red carpet. Leslee and her husband were still in their hotel room getting dressed when there was a knock on the door, and it was Nicole. She smiled and said, "Hi, are you ready? Want to have a glass of champagne?" She was early, looking beautiful, ready to go, and not waiting in her room for an entourage to accompany her. Leslee said this is just one example of what a supremely gracious and professional person Nicole Kidman is: "Nicole understands that part of her responsibility for making movies is to market them. I will tell you that what she does for a movie is extraordinary, consistently going way beyond the call of duty." I asked her for more details about what she meant. She said, "I'll explain to Nicole why she might have to make a grueling trip, or do just those few extra interviews, and once she understands the reasons, she may agree or disagree, but either way she's ready to go and that's that." Leslee said that there have been many times when it's been pouring down rain, bodyguards are manhandling her, but still Nicole will walk extra blocks and get soaking wet just to shake hands with her fans, or sign some extra autographs.

If the fabulous, couture-clad Nicole Kidman is willing to get soaking wet in order to shake the hands of a few more fans she'll probably never see again, shouldn't you be willing to go the extra mile to make sure that you give your customers perfect service or an extraordinary product? Nicole knows that every fan she meets is another ticket sold to her next film. And you should know that every customer you go out of your way for is another cupcake sold at your bakery.

Hard work must always be accompanied by persistence, which is key to any success. Rarely, if ever, does a first try result in success.

Take the case of Elisabeth Rohm, the actress who replaced Angie Harmon as Sam Waterston's cocounsel on *Law and Order*. Lis, like many aspiring actors and actresses, had to wait awhile for her big break, but she wasn't idle during that time. She went to countless auditions and practiced her craft endlessly, mostly without success. But she didn't see these rejections as failures; rather, she says the thing about life and seeking what you want is that "you can't pick and choose your battles—the whole thing is a battle . . . by definition, success is about endurance."

She had been taken on by a new agent and was visiting Los Angeles for a few days as a consequence. She had no expectation that she would be sent out for auditions during that short time, but surprisingly, she had a few. One of them was an audition for a Dick Wolf–produced pilot, which was the first time she met the man who would eventually become her *Law and Order* boss. She didn't get the pilot, but she made an impression on him.

When Wolf was looking to replace Carey Lowell on *Law and Order* some years later, Rohm again auditioned for Wolf. He once again liked her work, but the part ended up going to Angie Harmon. Another few years passed, and Angie Harmon was leaving the show. Once again Wolf needed a replacement. This time when Rohm auditioned, she got the part, and is now Waterston's co-star.

Ironically, something very similar happened to Rohm when it came to getting her first feature film role, in the forthcoming *Miss Congeniality 2*, starring Sandra Bullock. Rohm had auditioned for a part in *Miss Congeniality* but failed to get the role. This time around, when she was called to read for the part, she got it.

Lis points out that if she had let the first rejections really hurt her or deter her from continuing to put herself out there, she would never have gone back to re-audition in front of the very same people who didn't choose her the first time around. Needless to say, had she not done that, she wouldn't be where she is today. She knows that it takes persistence, a positive attitude, commitment, and extraordinary dedication to get ahead in any field, let alone in one where the competition is so steep, and the rejections so common.

When it comes to the meaning of hard work and persistence, even after you've hit the big time, I also think of someone like Candace Bushnell, who created *Sex and the City* with her *New York Observer* columns and later her book. She had hoped to be a children's book writer (she thought it was a more attainable goal than being a novelist, which was her dream). After toiling for more than a year over her first manuscript, it was rejected by every publisher she sent it to. She was earning a living as a freelance writer, but what kept her going was the idea of becoming a writer of books, not a columnist for a local weekly newspaper. Yet, what she was writing for the *Observer*, a hip, must-read periodical, was like nothing anyone had read before. She was giving readers a window into a fast-paced Manhattan life of parties, late-night clubs, friendships, and romances. For her first book, which was essentially a collection of columns, she received a modest advance from a good friend who ran a small but prestigious publishing house.

To promote the book, Candace made sure always to be seen by all the right people, in all the right places. Another friend, producer Darren Star, read her book and decided it would make a great television series, though admittedly, it was a gamble. Again, Candace received a modest advance—she wasn't sure the series would ever get made. In the interim she kept her nose to the grindstone and wrote her next work of fiction, comprising four novellas she titled *Four Blondes*. Around the same time it was published, the HBO series starring Sarah Jessica Parker came out and became a hit. Today Candace Bushnell is a celebrity. More important to her, however, is that she has achieved her dream, at the age of forty-five, of making her living as a novelist. She has a three-book contract with a major publishing house and is an internationally best-selling writer.

Whether it comes to the writing itself, or to the marketing of her books, Candace is a dedicated professional who works hard, is courteous and friendly when it comes to readers and fans, and knows that she must support her writing career with public appearances, autograph signings, and media appearances. Her attitude and commitment to what she does have been crucial to her success.

---

The Ohio Theory: Forget New York and Los Angeles. If something works in Ohio, it will be a national success. I will never forget the night six years ago when my daddy, born and bred in Cincinnati, stopped eating his dinner at the dining-room table and instead had it in front of the TV, in order to catch some guy named Bill O'Reilly on the boob tube. I should have known right then and there to buy stock in the Fox News Channel and Bill O'Reilly, because if Daddy's not eating at the table, then something is up! On a broader level, even if you are doing a national project, think of Ohio when bringing the plan together. It is the middle-class consumer who can make you a success. If you only focus on appealing to the elite, you will flop.

---

In another field, there is the success of Silvano Marchetto, owner of the now-legendary restaurant da Silvano, which lies in the heart of New York City's Greenwich Village. Silvano is a superb chef himself, and shops every day for the ingredients that are used in the day's meals. He has been in business for more than fifteen years, and for most of that time, the restaurant has been a destination for the city's movers and shakers, as well as many celebrities. Even visiting royalty can be spotted there. How has Silvano managed to attain this level of success, and to keep it up? For one, he is always present at the restaurant, meeting and greeting his patrons with a smile and a greeting (though, to tell the truth, at times it is almost impossible to understand what he is saying). No one knows how to work a room the way Silvano does. But he also knows the importance of getting publicity for the restaurant. You will frequently see mentions of da Silvano in Page Six, because there are so many nights when the list of patrons includes the likes of Jack Nicholson, Sean Penn, Gwyneth Paltrow, Rod Stewart, Bruce Willis, Sofia Coppola, and even yours truly. Silvano knows that being there to make sure that everything's working, that everyone is enjoying themselves, and that people who aren't there hear through the press and word of mouth what they're missing is as much a part of the formula for success as serving great food. His continuing love of the business, his positive attitude, and his dedication to keeping the restaurant running at a very high level combine to produce one of Manhattan's best-loved and most successful restaurants.

Some of what I'm telling you is common sense, just observing from my own daily experience that whether it's the manager of the place where I got my morning coffee or the hottest musician in the United States, getting and staying on top is never about just sitting there looking pretty. It's about passion, vision, dedication, and a belief in yourself and what you're doing, and the continuing knowledge that you need to be respectful of clients, fans—all of those who support your business, your craft. And that a job should always be done well and with professionalism. After all, you're getting (or going to get) paid for it!

## Chapter Three

# It's All About Timing and Location

SOMETIMES, THROUGH SHEER DUMB LUCK, COINCIDENCE, or the proper alignment of the stars (and this time I'm referring to the ones in the sky), everything just works out perfectly.

You plan your wedding (or someone else's, if you're a wedding planner like entertaining guru Jo Gartin), and you hold it outside, on the beach, no tent. The big day comes and the sky is beautiful, blue, cloudless. There is a light breeze, but just enough so that nothing blows off the tables, skirts stay in place, hats stay on heads. Ordinarily, there is the din of traffic in the background, but today, for some inexplicable reason, it is quiet. Typically on a warm summer day, your hair gets very frizzy, but today it falls gently into calm ringlets. Your dog isn't

73

even barking, though there are tons of people around. Everyone is on time, the ceremony comes off without a hitch, you have even managed to enjoy yourself. You breathe a sigh of relief, and now on to the honeymoon!

Okay, that is the fairy tale. Most of the time, let's face it, if you fail to order a tent, it rains. The minister gets lost on the way to the ceremony, and ends up being two hours late. The dog jumps up on your Vera Wang dress and gets muddy paw prints all over it. Your hair is a fuzzy mess. Perhaps all this would just be bad luck, but more likely, it would mean that you didn't plan properly for all the contingencies. Your timing was bad (you scheduled your wedding near Fenway Park at the same time a Red Sox game is set to begin), and your choice of location (you picked an historic church that was under massive reconstruction) was clearly poor.

A wedding planner would have known how to avoid these pitfalls, but had you done your homework, thought strategically, and planned properly, you too could have concluded that it would be better to have your wedding at your second location choice, and at a time that would enable guests, family, and wedding party to arrive on schedule.

When it comes to launching a business, pursuing a

new job, throwing a party, staging an art opening or band appearance—when it comes to just about anything in life, timing and location are critically important. If you are planning to approach your boss about a raise, is it smart to do it when you are at the annual holiday party and it's unlikely she wants to talk about business (or will even remember it in the morning)? Or to walk into a boss's office, find him with his head in his hands muttering to himself about his absurd mortgage rates, but decide to go ahead and do what you came in for, which was to ask for a six-month leave of absence? That would be suicidal. When it comes to any important one-on-one conversation, it's necessary to think ahead. At what time of day is your boss most relaxed and open? Is it better to have a vital conversation with him in the office, where he might be distracted by phone calls, e-mail, and other interruptions? Would it be better to make an appointment, or to risk catching him off guard? Is it possible to invite him out for a quiet lunch and then approach him with your question?

When it comes to embarking on the path to fame and fortune, it's important to think about how, when, and where to start. In the real estate business, the mantra is "location, location, location." But how important is location in the quest for success in whatever you are attempting? How important is timing? In my mind, both things are equally crucial. For example, as I mention elsewhere in the book, there are certain months of the year that are ideal for certain types of publicity.

---

Sometimes location is enough. Jeanie Buss is the executive vice president of business operations for the Los Angeles Lakers. (She also happens to be the owner's daughter.) Jeanie laughed when I asked her about location making you famous and said, "Holding Laker floor seats can make you famous. *Vanity Fair* had a story on who sits on the floor at Laker games. So if you can score floor seats, people who attend the games, who watch on TV, scan that one row of seats and try to figure out who everybody is.

"There's one guy who sits a few seats away from Jack Nicholson who is just this outrageous dresser. Snakeskin, matching snakeskin pants and jacket, and a hat with a feather coming off of it. It's just so eccentric, and he always draws attention, and people always ask me, Who is he? Meaning, he's famous, right? And everyone thinks he must be a music industry executive, something in the entertainment industry, because who else could dress like that? Turns out he owns real estate, and the real estate he owns is mobile homes. His name is Jimmy Goldstein. I cannot tell you, people always ask me. They're waiting for some great story, like he discovered Madonna or something.

"But Jimmy's found a way to become a member of an inner circle that he normally wouldn't be a part of, because he sits on the floor. He's a perfect example of becoming a celebrity really for no reason other than location. People will do anything to get seats on the floor. A few years ago, there was a recording artist who hadn't done anything for about ten years, he kind of had fallen through the cracks. I can't use his name. Someone had returned two floor seats to me that they weren't using. I said, 'Hey, if you want to come to a Laker game, I have two floor seats.' He ended up sitting on the floor, a record producer was at the game, went down and said, 'Hey, how you doing, I haven't seen you in ten years, what's going on?' This guy said, 'I've been working on some new music, written some stuff.' The guy goes, 'I would love to hear it.' He ended up getting a record deal out of it, and I got a nice bouquet of flowers.

"And remember, Paula Abdul was a Laker girl. I don't remember which Jackson family member it was, maybe it was a couple of them, were sitting on the floor at a Laker game and they saw Paula dancing and it started her career."

Now, while you may not live in Los Angeles or know Jeanie, there are always places in even the smallest town to go to be seen and noticed and to mingle with people who can help you and your career. Find them!

---

In the world of book publishing, for example, September and October are considered months for bringing out books by the most-established writers, who will do well if competing for shelf space with others. Publishers know that in an election year, it is death to bring out a work of serious nonfiction that is unrelated to the election just before or after Election Day because the media will be consumed with election news and therefore less likely to devote any coverage to the book. The *Today* show is not going to have the author on then, because they will be looking for guests who can fill their need for harder news.

On the other hand, November is the ideal time to publish a big, expensive coffee-table book on Italy (makes a good holiday gift), and January is the perfect time to bring out a health or diet book that answers the demand for helping to achieve New Year's resolutions, such as "I am going to start exercising this year" or "I am going to lose ten pounds this year."

As for publicists who are trying to break out new products, or get lots of coverage for an event that may not be a slam dunk in terms of publicity, January and August are considered slow news months, therefore chances are better in those months of getting someone in the media to pay attention since there is less competition to fill air time or print space. A publicist in Miami, for example, told me that Miami's "high" season is getting shorter and shorter. The high season is in the winter months, when people from all over the States and the world flock to Miami, escaping their cold climates to soak up some sun and have some fun. With such a high concentration of boldfaced names, and the subsequent media attention, everyone is jamming in as many high-profile celebrity-driven parties and corporate events as possible.

---

High Season in Florida is in winter. Starting in November, many well-heeled New Yorkers and

Angelenos will pack up and jet down to South Beach and Palm Beach to fill up the cities' hottest hotels. The season ends in late January or early February. The original "season" was much longer, starting in September and lasting through March. Due to other hot spots such as Mexico and Brazil popping up, the Miami season has been cut short.

---

Clearly, then, it would be in your interest to schedule a launch event or party in Miami during the low-season months, maybe right before winter hits, or in spring when there is still a cold blast in New York, when local media would be hungrier for news, and when there is not such intense competition for the media's time.

If you are thinking about launching a new business, starting a new venture, or reinventing—or even inventing—yourself, and you have not already decided on where to take the plunge, consider all your options carefully. If you are willing to relocate to another city, pick a city that needs your services. When I was going to college in Atlanta in the early nineties, Atlanta was growing at a huge rate, so fast that its nickname was "Hotlanta." Restaurants and bars popped up everywhere, and it was an ideal time for, say, a dry-cleaning company or a company that services linens, to move to that city and offer the best deal around in tablecloth cleaning.

Almost every year, business magazines publish lists of the nation's fastest-growing cities or best places to live. Pick one and then ask yourself, "Do I know anyone in the area to ease my transition?" Other questions to ask: Does the area have any amenities I will need? How much competition in my field will I face? What does the competition specialize in? Are my neighbors desirable, or will they graffiti my store every night? Is there enough parking in the area?

These types of questions can be answered with a trip to a public library or by going online and doing some research on the Internet. It is also a good idea to check out any potential business partners with the Better Business Bureau, and to contact other local business owners about your particular concerns.

Now, if you are not prepared to move, start looking at growth areas or up-and-coming neighborhoods in your own town. Beware, however, that if the area has been up-and-coming for more than five years, chances are it came and went.

The same questions that apply if you were moving to another city also apply to moving to a new area in your current city or town. Say you are looking to launch a new clothing line, and the clothes are very cutting edge, or even outrageous. You haven't yet decided on whether to open the business in your hometown of Atlanta or to migrate to a city that is more of a fashion capital, such as New York or L.A. If you were to stay in Atlanta, you would have the advantage of knowing your home turf, of knowing who the city's "bigmouths" are, of knowing which of Atlanta's neighborhoods are most affordable and most conducive to business. Presumably you already have connections in the fashion community and in the fashion press, and therefore know the right people to invite to your debut fashion show, store opening, and the like.

On the other hand, Atlanta PR maven Liz Lapidus describes Atlanta's fashion scene as being less forward-thinking than other cities. She says that unlike New York or Los Angeles, in Atlanta you "can wear last season and still be fashionable." So perhaps this means that Atlanta's shoppers might not be receptive to your more progressive fashions, and that you would instead find a niche in a city where avant-garde is good. Then again, you could move to a funky area of the city, like Little Five Points, and start dressing the more urban, chic Atlantans.

How do you figure out what's best for you if you

don't have ready access to the city's top publicist? Start by reading the city's local magazines and small-press papers to see what's being featured, and to see what the local celebrities are wearing. Do your homework, and know the necessary questions to ask for your business. If you are trying to break into a local television market, what are your chances if you don't have much prior experience? If you choose a smaller market, your chances will likely be better. If you are looking to launch a coffee bar, don't choose a town that has a Starbucks on every corner. Or, if you have your heart set on taking on Starbucks, make sure your product is better, cheaper, and faster. Or look either to offer something that isn't already offered there or to break into a neighborhood that is just beginning to be gentrified. But the key is to know your stuff. Talk to the local Chamber of Commerce. Do your own shoe-leather research. Find out what the economic composition of your target neighborhood is, and figure out whether your service is a good fit with that population.

MTV's Jillian Kogan notes that in L.A., outrageous is no problem: "L.A. is such a wonderful place . . . it doesn't matter how ridiculous an outfit is . . . or how much cleavage is showing—it works." New York, on the other hand, is not only tough to break into, but it is also very label-conscious. Stylish New York women favor labels like Prada, Marc Jacobs, Roberto Cavalli, and other established designers. Even hot young designers like Zac Posen usually get embraced only after a handful of celebrities have adopted the line and been photographed for the pages of *People*, *US Weekly*, and *Star* magazines. Then impressionable, fashion-conscious women flock to the stores in order to mimic their fashion icons.

---

Figure out in which city or neighborhood your kind of business or profession already attracts the most customers, and the least. Then go somewhere in the middle so you can fill a niche *and* make money.

---

In terms of getting media coverage, location can often be used to great advantage. For the New York premiere of the Howard Stern movie *Private Parts*, Dan Klores had the idea of drawing Stern fans to a huge screening in the way fans of a rock band are drawn to a concert. The film's release was scheduled for February, so he knew an outdoor venue wasn't possible. From his perspective, then, the only other perfect, fabulous location would be Madison Square Garden. But at first he couldn't talk the executives at Paramount into this idea. Gradually, though, he convinced them that tying a Madison Square Garden concert-type premiere to the launch of a CD soundtrack at city record stores would have the effect of blanketing the city with buzz about the *Private Parts* extravaganza. The strategy worked.

When I consider the importance of location, I always think about the restaurateur Danny Meyer, whose five New York restaurants have all been incredible successes, beginning with the now classic Union Square Cafe, consistently voted New York City's most popular restaurant in *Zagat*. In many ways, Danny is a visionary, but his choice of location has been a consistent key to his success. He chose to locate Union Square Cafe, his first restaurant, in the Flatiron District, a neighborhood that was a little down at the heels at the time, believing that he could be a part of the area's revitalization. His gamble paid off. His restaurant was good enough to pull customers in from all parts of the city, and it became one of the neighborhood's anchors, reassuring other potential area investors that they too could find success there.

His four other restaurants are pretty much within walking distance of that first one, and today the area is home to many great restaurants, some of the best in the city.

Some of the greatest innovators of our time have filled a niche, launching a brand-new idea at what seems like exactly the right time, taking advantage of "timing" in a way that is simply ingenious, that not only fills a need, but which also actually creates a need for a previously nonexistent product. Take Ted Turner, founder of CNN, or Bill Gates, founder of Microsoft. These two men had visionary ideas that they were able to translate into practical commodities, and then were able to launch them at what, in retrospect, seems like precisely the right moment.

I wouldn't put reality-television-show innovator Mark Burnett into quite the same category as Ted Turner or Bill Gates, but Burnett's ventures also illustrate good timing. Burnett saw that network television programming was becoming a bit stale, and that for many networks, conventional drama or sitcom formulas just weren't working anymore. Now Burnett's productions, from *Survivor* to *The Apprentice* to *The Restaurant*, make up an entire category of television unto themselves, providing programming that is integral to several networks' primetime schedules.

---

Remember, imitation is the sincerest form of flattery. You may be first on the block, but you won't be the last. Just be the best, and you will dominate your industry.

---

So how does all this apply to you? Say you are launching a small business in your hometown. Is there a particularly important season for your business, one that makes it essential for you to be out there along with your competitors during that season? If you are a florist, for example, and you are aiming for a high-end clientele who throw a lot of parties, when is the "high season" for parties in your city? There are always lots of holiday parties in December, but when does the planning for them begin? If you want to be considered for those holiday parties, is it too early to start thinking about outreach to possible clients as early as the spring? What is the best way to reach those clients? How do you ensure that they know about you, that they have had the chance to see your work? Perhaps you have a family friend who is well established in the city society circles. Persuade her to host a party to introduce you. You can finance the party, and of course provide the floral arrangements. Perhaps there is a worthy organization that is planning an event, but because it is a nonprofit, it doesn't have a lot to spend on things like flowers, but you know that lots of A-listers will be in attendance. Offer to do the flowers at a very discounted rate, even if it means losing money on the event. Be sure you have plenty of business cards on hand the night of the event, and also make sure to look at the guest list ahead of time to find out about any VIPs and press who will be in attendance. Make sure the invitation has a line reading, "Flowers designed by . . ."

Desiree Gruber, founder and CEO of the PR firm Full Picture, also recognizes the importance of timing to her public relations business and to her clients. She says, "it's all about knowing who your consumer is, and knowing when that consumer is most likely to be receptive to your product."

For years Desiree has masterminded the Victoria's Secret fashion show extravaganzas with extraordinary creativity, and with great results. The shows have been staged at various times, depending on the company's goals for that year. For example, one year the show was timed for Valentine's Day. According to Gruber, "Victoria's Secret wanted to *own* Valentine's Day that year." The event was planned not only with an eye toward getting shoppers to purchase Victoria's Secret lingerie for the holiday, but also to maximize press coverage. The models all wore items that were tied thematically to the holiday. Backstage, they made ten supermodels available to the press, who asked such hard-hitting questions as "What will you wear on Valentine's Day?" and "What are you hoping to get as a Valentine's Day gift?" Naturally, the interviews, as well as the show itself, got a ton of media attention.

But Gruber makes a larger point. She observes that everything is cyclical, like action movie blockbusters, which are released in the summer because their target teenage market is out of school and available to spend its dollars at the box office. "The social season," she observes, "occurs in the fall, which is why months before, socialites are chatting by phone and e-mail, figuring out when to hold their various parties, galas, and balls, so that their dates don't conflict."

When considering how to apply this sort of thinking to your own endeavor, just take it one step at a time. What are your goals? Who do you have to enlist to help achieve them, and what is your best chance of getting them on board, whether it's the press, your friends, your family, or your investors? Have you given thought to what impact your choice of location will have on your plans? That could determine whether you launch your acting career in L.A., New York, or Chicago, or it could influence when and where you will kick off your campaign to become P.T.A. president. Even U.S. presidents and former presidents take this into account—Bill Clinton rushed to finish his 2004 autobiography so its publication wouldn't distract from the Democratic National Convention and the election itself. Have you done your homework?

## Chapter Four

# Do You Have the Look?

THERE ARE VERY FEW PEOPLE OUT THERE, AND THAT IN-cludes the fabulously famous few in New York and Los Angeles, who don't need a little bit of a makeover every now and then. I'm not talking about an extreme, change-everything-about-yourself with the help of a plastic surgeon and the staff of a network television makeover show—although some people could use that. I'm talking about making the most of what you've got.

Take my friend Dianne, for example.

Dianne is a powerful television producer. At any given moment she has five shows in production and two already on the air. She's an attractive woman, but half the time you would never know it. Her hair is always pulled back in a messy ponytail, more often than not she shows up at work or events wearing a sweat suit, and she almost never wears makeup. I will always remember the day I forced her to go to a real hairdresser, to put on some stylish clothes, and to try a little makeup—she was unrecognizable and gorgeous, and most important, instead of looking like the office intern, she looked like the executive in charge. If she came to work like that every day, I have no doubt but that she would be running the entire network!

As shallow as it sounds, I think we all know that looks are important. Uber-publicist Matthew Rich is fond of saying, "It's a proven fact that the better-looking person gets the job." That's what I'm talking about. Let's get that job!

So how do you figure out what your best assets are and how do you accentuate them and play down your flaws? If you can't assess your own attributes, ask an expert, but choose that person wisely. Don't appoint the clerk with the big hair down at the corner drugstore to be your personal style guru. Ask some people whose opinions you value what they think your best qualities are.

Does everyone tell you that you have an incredible smile, or that you have gorgeous hair, or that you look great in red? Make a list of what you have to offer in the plus column, and then start building a foundation for your new, updated look from there. This can be as simple as doing some research on who gives the best haircut in town for the money, or finding a signature clothing style and sticking with it so that people begin to identify you with it. Use fashion magazines but don't be a slave to them—just because you're not model-thin doesn't mean you can't look great (who the hell wants to look like a twelve-year-old boy anyway?) and I don't want to tell you what I've learned while being an entertainment reporter about what some models do to stay so skinny!!! Want to look like Cameron Diaz? Did you know that she has one of the worst cases of adult acne I've ever seen? However, this doesn't seem to stop certain fashion magazines from describing her skin as "glowing." The point of this is not to pick on Cameron Diaz but to illustrate that what you see in magazines is often more about airbrushing and camera trickery than it is about what people really look like. (I know for a fact that J.Lo and even bone-thin Lara Flynn Boyle have cellulite!)

And there is always the example of Jennifer Aniston. In 2004 she graced the cover of *People* magazine's "Most Beautiful People" issue. But is she really beautiful, or just extremely well groomed? When she first started out, Jen was, if not homely, certainly no one you'd look twice at. But after getting expensive highlights in her hair, teeth whitening, eyebrow waxing, correct makeup, a great diet and trainer, and superb clothes, she's been transformed—without plastic surgery—into a swan.

WIRE IMAGE

WIRE IMAGE

ZUNA PRESS

The same can be said about Jennifer Lopez. Her best friends are clearly her eyebrow waxer and her StairMaster. The point is, you too can go from dull to heavenly with some hard work and expert help.

The magic of a great eyebrow wax: There is nothing more life-changing than a good eyebrow

RETNA

WIRE IMAGE

wax. Eyebrows frame your face, and if properly groomed, can instantly give you a good, clean look. Believe me—I come from sturdy Southern Italian and Eastern European stock. The hairy part of Eastern Europe. My sisters and I didn't find out the wonders of freeing ourselves from our uni-brow chains until we were well into our twenties, and are so much better-looking for it. I'd show you the before and after family portraits, but well, it's too embarrassing, and why look at me when you can check out bushy-browed Jennifer Lopez's transformation into thin-arched-brow diva?

---

AND repeat after me: Anorexia is not pretty. Bulimia gives you bad breath. Being a size zero means you are underweight and scrawny. Adult acne happens, and so does the emergence of a pear-shaped body after age thirty. Your imperfections are often what make you endearing. (Except for one particularly notable weight gain I went through after quitting smoking for the third time. I ended up naming my thighs the thunder twins. They were scary, but we got along. Hell—we had to: I was going to bed with them every night and waking up with them every morning.)

So after you've figured out what parts of yourself you can live with and what needs a bit of a touch-up, you're on your way.

One more aside: your goal should not be to look like Uma Thurman if you are short with curly dark hair. (Let's face it: Most of us will never look like Uma Thurman no matter how hard we try, so why have something impossible like that in mind?) Anyway, most of the people you see in magazines, on TV, or in the movies, the ones who always look fantastic even when they are just hanging out—well guess what? That "ain't it easy?" look takes HOURS of time. There are actually machines that spray on paint foundation, and assistants who help them apply fake eye-lashes—sometimes even made of mink. And that's in between trips to the toilet because the laxatives are starting to kick in.

And don't think the male celebrities are any different. When I say waxing, that goes for the guys as well. Half of the Hollywood Boys Club has had their hair plucked, waxed, and lasered off. And need I say *manscaping*? The art of spraying fake tan on the stomach to create abs is very popular.

Back on planet earth, looking fabulous is not simply a matter of waking up, taking a shower, and heading out the door. Anyone who tells you otherwise is either lying or under the age of fourteen! For me and most everyone else I know, including those famous "it" girls who populate the city of New York, getting ready in the morning or preparing to go out at night is hard work! Putting one's face on takes time. I've gotten it down to as fast as fifteen minutes, but that's for my semi-human, not entirely alien look.

Heed this battle cry to get off your ass and become proactive about your appearance, about the way you present yourself, and resolve to do what it takes to go from mousy to magnificent. Looking the part can get you just about anywhere, and persuade anyone to take a chance on you!

What happened to me is illustrative. Before Page Six, I worked for Dow Jones Newswires, where I wrote about interest-rate swaps and over-the-counter derivatives (obscure financial transactions). At Dow few people cared what I—or they, for that matter—looked like, as long as I adhered to their stiflingly dull wardrobe requirements (bland suit, bland blouse, and—yuck—pumps).

That all changed once I arrived at the *New York Post*'s Page Six, where I was required to go out every night. Granted, because of my job, no one was going to deny me admission to their event, because, let's face it, they wanted to get into the paper. Still, I knew the way I looked would have a lot to do with how people treated me. But it wasn't until I started being asked to comment on the entertainment business for television that I fully realized that a shower and a shake were no longer going to do it for me.

I was the new kid on the block at Page Six, and as such, a lot of the TV stations wanted to try me out as an "expert" on the celebrity beat. Have you ever seen yourself on TV? I found out right away that the camera tends to accentuate the awful and minimize the great. Prior to that, I'd had no idea that when my hair was in its naturally curly, frizzy state, I looked like a walking Q-tip.

Besides the fact that I didn't know how to do my hair or makeup or style my clothes for television, there was also the problem that I wasn't that good at talking on the air right away, but that's a story for another chapter. For a while, the calls stopped coming in. But then I figured it out, and something changed. I started getting my hair blown out. And this is a side note for all you curly girls out there: Curly hair is great, cool, wonderful, etc., but it does *not* translate well on the small screen without a team of stylists backing you up.

---

TV Trannie: The look we all have after coming off a TV shoot. To look good on the tube, you literally have to spackle it on. Never, and I mean NEVER, go on TV without makeup. You will look washed out, tired, and freakish. Now, please note, this will make you look good on TV, but in real life: TONE IT DOWN! There is a time and place for the TV Tranny, and girlfriend, it ain't at a cocktail party or PTA meeting. Don't overdo the makeup. If you accidentally wipe the sleeve of your white shirt against your face or forehead and it comes away brown with foundation, we have a problem.

---

I began paying attention to what the station's makeup people did to my face and copied their moves. With my hair and makeup under control, it was time to think about what colors were good for television (bright ones) and start wearing them. It may sound very Stepford, but it helped get me a contract with *Entertainment Tonight.* Now my momma and daddy, along with 9 million other people, can see me once a week!

My friend Matthew Rich advocates cultivating your

own unique look to stand out, the way Andy Warhol did with a few pairs of black jeans and a wig. "It's all about self-branding," says Matthew. Take Mary McFadden, a famous fashion designer who is one of his clients. Early in her life—she's of a certain age now—Mary adopted a very severe look: white pancake makeup, rice powder, and a blunt pageboy haircut with the hair dyed jet black. One day she will be 110 years old, and people who knew her when will look at her and say, "Oh my God, you have not changed a bit!"

Okay, so now let's take it step by step.

## 1. Grooming

---

Pulling an Ethan (as in Hawke), also known as pulling a Jared (as in Leto): There are very few people who can pull off the dirty, grungy look. And even fewer who can pull it off without smelling like last week's socks. Let me give you a hint: You are not one of the few. And if you think you are, snap out of it! Unless you are in high school, very few people actually find this "look" attractive. Hell, just ask Uma Thurman. When she ditched Ethan, she ran straight to the arms of hotelier Andre Balazs, a slim, sleek man, who *always* bathes and shaves!

---

If you're reading this book, I hope you will think that much of what is in this section is glaringly, painfully obvious. For example, I hope I don't have to tell you to TAKE A SHOWER! Whether you are man, woman, or child, unless you live in France, remember: Cleanliness is fundamental. Looking a little rough around the edges is just a style. Appearing as if you just got out of bed can look sexy and sultry, but really just getting out of bed and throwing some toothpaste across your teeth with your finger and then running out the door is seriously unattractive. So even if your individual look is I-don't-spend-any-time-at-all-on-how-I-look messy, be sure that there is no dirt under your fingernails, that the grease in your hair comes only from your styling gel, that those ratty-looking jeans are clean and ratty-looking. If your favorite white shirt has pit stains, get rid of it! If your beloved vintage Gucci shoes have worn-down heels and are unraveling from the top down, take them to the shoemaker or retire them! Pay attention to the details that signal to others that you take care with your appearance.

### 2. Hair

My friend Ken Cranford is a forty-two-year-old scissor master at the Stephen Knoll Salon in New York City. He speaks the truth when he says, "A woman can go out and spend a thousand dollars on clothing, but she's not going to have 'the look' if her hair doesn't go with it."

I myself have struggled mightily to get my hair to behave, and so I asked Ken to tell me more. "Hair needs to be treated as an accessory, just like anything else," he told me.

"People fail to realize this, and go out and spend two hundred or more on a blouse and then go to some inexpensive salon and have their hair cut. You've got hair twenty-four seven, and if it doesn't look good, you are stuck with it. So I would rather spend the money on the basics, the hair. The blouse is dispensable."

Once you've come to grips with the fact that your hair will never look like Christie Brinkley's (or at least not without the daily help of a team of stylists), take a deep breath and look closely at the shape of your face, consider the type of hair you have, your age, what look will enhance your best features. Ken told me, "I have transformed plenty of clients . . . by having a little more height, less volume on the sides." Little things go a long way to creating a whole look.

I know it may seem shallow to have an entire discussion about hair, but you and I both know that a good cut can make a woman look younger, thinner, taller—even transform or define her career (as in Jennifer Aniston, Farrah Fawcett, or—remember Dorothy Hamill?).

---

The emotional cut: Honey, we have all been there. I used to take the approach, "I'm gonna cut that man right out of my hair" when I had broken up with someone. Which is how, at the age of twenty-two, I ended up looking like a fuzzy Q-tip. It had been a particularly busy (and bad) man-year. I now get highlights instead. Which is always much saner and, well, my roots need to be touched up every three months anyhow. But the point is, steer clear of a salon if anything bad is going on. Edward Scissorhands at Supercuts doesn't have to live with that ill-advised shag mullet, you do.

---

However, beware of the emotional cut. You know what I'm talking about. It's the old "my man left me, my work sucks, my mortgage is killing me and I need a change" cut. Ken advises, "That's actually fine for a change. But knowing my clients as I do, I know some of the changes they're responding to are not going to be permanent. In that case I say, 'I don't do emotional haircuts.' Because I know one week later she's going to come back to me and yell: 'What were you thinking!? You know me!!'"

And for you guys out there, unless you're Donald Trump, a signature comb-over is a no-no. Bald is always better than wearing some obvious toupee (and trust me they're all obvious), and there are few bigger turn-offs than middle-aged men wearing their hair in a ponytail.

Not everyone is lucky enough to know Ken (or to be able to afford him, for that matter). So what do you do if you can't afford the best hairstylist in town, or live in a place that doesn't have the top cutters flocking to it? In almost every major city there is a Vidal Sassoon, an Aveda, or another good "brand" salon, and if you can't afford the top person there, they often offer trainees who are willing to cut (with supervision) for as little as $25. Find a place you like, find the cut that works for you, and you're halfway there.

Now we come to the tricky question of color. Doing your color at home is not the optimum choice, but if you can't afford to have a salon colorist do it, choose your brand carefully—my favorite New York colorist, also at Stephen Knoll Salon, Rita Starnella, recommends Clairol Natural Instincts. But she offers this advice: Never go more than two shades lighter or darker, and if you're going to dye your hair at home, just do the overall color, not highlights.

In general, says my colorist Rita, who has worked with such fashionistas as Anna Wintour and Pamela Fiori, the editor of *Town & Country*, "You should go lighter as you get older. A little bit at a time. Remember Johnny Cash, with his black hair, and Wayne Newton? They looked horrible . . . like Morticia Addams. So I start taking my clients lighter and lighter . . . it softens them up."

There are countless drugstore products that cost a fraction of Rita's $250 highlights (which are, however, amazing and worth every penny). She suggests sticking to products that say they are "deposit only" color, and staying away from anything that says "peroxide." She also advises staying away from the "paint kits" where you pull sections of hair through holes in a scalp covering—they will produce hair that is blotchy and altogether awful-looking. If you do mess up, Rita says the only way to fix it yourself is to "throw something over it. Like a brown, if your hair is brown to begin with. Just cover it up!"

### 3. Skin

---

Recommended grooming products: After years of trying out everything under the sun, here's my list of products that work. Skin: For those of you not on a tight budget, stick to the "La's," as in La Mer and La Prairie. Kiehl's does a good cream with powder in it to stop shine, the entire line of Mario Badescu is amazing, and for those who still shop at Rite Aid, Pond's cold cream still works wonders, as do Neutrogena, Oil of Olay, and plain old Vaseline. As for hair, after all these years, I still can't find a better-smelling or -acting product than Pantene Pro-V. And for all you smokers out there, they now have hair sprays that will cover up the smoke smell. Use them. The stale smoke smell is so yesterday. Literally.

---

There is nothing like clear, clean, glowing skin (unless it's clean, shiny hair) to signal health, beauty, and attractiveness. I will never forget when I quit smoking. After a month or so people began stopping me on the street just to comment on how great I looked.

This was significant for me not only because I had quit smoking (sadly, I am back on the habit), but also because I had suffered—oh, how I had suffered—from acne as a teenager and still suffer the occasional outbreak. But had I known as a teenager that with just a few simple changes of my daily routine I could have had great skin all along, it would have saved me a lot of heartache!

Which brings me to skin-care rule number one, a rule I intend to follow soon (but for now do as I say and not as I do!): Quit smoking!

For advice about skin I turned to a man who has worked with Courteney Cox Arquette, Rene Russo, Heidi Klum, and Stephanie Seymour, among many others.

He is the skin guru of our time, with lines of best-selling books and skin products: Nicholas Perricone, author of *The Acne Prescription*. The first thing he does is to put people on the "three-day nutritional face-lift." He instructs readers and clients to eat plenty of salmon, green salad with oil and lemon juice, and berries or melon. Because these foods act as natural anti-inflammatories, they produce radiant skin in just a few days. He also urges clients to give up coffee and replace it with green tea, and to drink ten glasses of water a day.

But Dr. Perricone, like many other skin specialists, knows it is not just about what you eat and drink (although this is a huge factor). Developing a great complexion also requires reducing stress as much as possible, and therefore he recommends 15 to 20 minutes of yoga per day, which will serve to increase circulation, lower the levels of "bad" hormones, and promote better sleep.

Perricone does not recommend a complicated skin regimen of expensive creams and cleansers. He suggests "a mild cleanser, followed by an anti-inflammatory cream with alpha lipoic acids, all of which are natural and can be found in health food stores." (One such product is DMAE, a concentrate of a natural substance found in fish that can also be found in health food stores.) He says, "All the stars use DMAE on their faces. No matter how bad a night you have had, you'll look good."

Okay, now we've conquered basic grooming, hair, and skin. On to my favorite topic (yum!) . . .

## 4. Clothes

There is a wonderful book by Kim France & Andrea L., the editor and creative director of the magazine *Lucky,* called *The Lucky Shopping Manual.* It's great because it tells women, and more important, shows them, how best to dress given their particular body issues, whether that might be a small or large bust, big thighs, small ass, no waistline, etc. I recommend you check this book out if you need help figuring out how to revamp your wardrobe to suit your shape.

How can you look the part without spending exorbitant amounts of money? I love the idea of the "capsule wardrobe" supplemented by pieces you know always look good on you.

According to stylists Jesse Garza and Joe Lupo, who run the nationally famous Visual Therapy and do a lot of work for the *Oprah* show, it all comes down to buying good basics. They advise their clients, who include some of the best-groomed men and women in the entire country, to purchase a capsule wardrobe. The specifics vary from person to person, but always include a few key pieces around which an entire wardrobe can be built. This could mean investing in a great Armani suit, in two pairs of carefully chosen, expensive shoes, three or four different tops or shirts to wear with the suit (and a few well chosen ties if you are a guy), a great purse, and an evening bag. Everything else you purchase will augment or relate to this basic capsule. It will be your "go to" outfit to be worn whenever you need to look your best, or don't know what else to wear.

---

The best beauty magazines: Now I am not talking aspirational beauty mags like *Vogue*, where every dress is $10,000. The magazines that are most helpful for women on a budget are *Lucky*, *Marie Claire*, *Cosmopolitan*, *Glamour*, and *Real Simple*. All of these magazines show you how to shop for basics while mixing and matching. As for internal beauty and mental health, there is no better than Oprah's mag, *O!* Damned if that woman can't make any batch of lemons into a good vat of lemonade.

---

Garza and Lupo recommend starting this process by "editing your closet," which means taking a good, hard look at what you have and deciding whether you are still wearing it and if it still works as a component of your wardrobe. If it doesn't, either "demote" the item to around the house loungewear, or give it away. The point is to figure out what the best look is for you, to clarify what "type" you are—the Visual Therapy team breaks this down into four types: classic, chic, avant-garde, and bohemian. Then find the pieces that work to bring out your best characteristics, and get rid of those that cry out "from college" or "yesterday."

What are examples of good basics? According to Couri Hay, this could be as simple as finding a good pair of jeans and a great T-shirt. "Then add a cool pair of stilettos, or a cute pair of boots. Then, maybe a good blazer." He thinks that good taste is all around us now, and that often, it's surprisingly cheap. He observes that even Karl Lagerfeld, Chanel's design chief, said that thanks to stores like the Gap, "there's no excuse to be badly dressed. There's Martha Stewart at Kmart, Isaac Mizrahi at Target, so there's no excuse for you not to have clean lines . . . good lines in your home. The reality is, good taste is all around you. You just have to find it." Even Lagerfeld himself has now designed a cheap line for discount retailer H&M.

I have to admit I am an eBay junkie. To date, I have bought my car (a 1974 Dodge Dart Swinger for $750), five pairs of Manolo Blahniks, six purses, and a variety of great clothing on eBay. The best way to shop online is seasonally, after designers like Dolce

& Gabbana, Chanel, Prada, and Valentino have had their sales. Apparently lots of women shop until they drop in the spring, summer, and fall and then make up for what they've spent by reselling their now unwanted treasures on eBay.

In September 2003, the *New York Post* did a cheapie shopping spree on eBay and found a $2000 Armani dress selling for $299, a $1695 Helmut Lang tuxedo suit also for under $300, an $800 Louis Vuitton bag for $500, and $800 Manolo boots for $295.

Personally, I also love the sample sales we are lucky to have all over New York City. I once snapped up an $8000 Dolce mink for $900. I didn't eat for two weeks, but it was worth it! For those of you who don't live in New York—many of those sample-sale goodies sold in late spring and fall can be found on eBay.

When to shop online or otherwise. The major designers, including Prada, Dolce & Gabbana, Chanel, and Diane von Furstenburg all have sample sales in the late spring, around the end of May, and in the fall, near the end of September or October. Sample sales are when the designers dump product that either didn't sell or never went fully to market. To get rid of the clothes, in order to make room for the next season, the designers will sell them at severely reduced prices, sometimes up to 90 percent off. Many of these unused clothes will make their way onto eBay. If you don't want to shop the Internet, try your local high-end retailer. After Christmas, before the New Year, the sales are astronomical—also, at the end of summer. Check with your favorite store to find out exactly when their big sales take place. They will have had the sale dates on the calendar for a year. By doing this, you can get high-end, great-quality clothes for a fraction of the cost, and sometimes, the high-end sale items are cheaper than the local discount stores—although the lure and value of places like Target and TJ Maxx and Loehmann's should never be underrated.

You don't have to live in a big city to find great bargains in consignment and vintage shops. There is nothing like stumbling on a great Pucci blouse for $10, or finding a sweet little Chanel jacket for a mere $40 to make the search worth it!

Remember, too, that the most expensive store in

town can become the cheapest during summer clearance sales, and during the period between Christmas and New Year's. And there is also something to be said for good, old-fashioned detective work when it comes to masterful clothes shopping.

A friend of mine named Carlota Espinosa, who is a fashion producer for Fox 11 in L.A., offered this tip: Ask someone you know who is always well dressed where they shop, and they will no doubt tell you about a new place you've never heard of before. She was turned on by a friend to a place called Govinda's, which is a Hare Krishna–run thrift shop. "You literally can get a pashmina for fifty percent of the usual price. I walked in there and saw a bunch of stylists and celebrities. Or a friend told me about a shoe place right in the heart of Beverly Hills, but it's not a store—it's an office. They have shoes from Italy at half the price. There's a ton of stuff like that, you just gotta find it."

---

Barter your way into a discount: What if you love a particular store, but it is very expensive? If it is family owned, and not a chain, get to know the owners and see if you can barter a service of yours, such as floral design, for a discount. If it is a larger store, ask if they have a preferred-customer program. Remember, just as with upgrades at an airline, you won't get if you don't ask.

---

The bottom line is to know yourself, do everything that you can to make the most of your best features and do your homework in terms of styles, trends, and designers. There is a fine line between being fashionable and being a slave to fashion. I suggest employing style gurus Garza and Lupo's "value equation," which helps a consumer to figure out if the quality of an item justifies its price. Is it going to be outdated next season? If so, be sure you have the money to burn, and that you love it enough to make a purchase that may have to be retired to the back of the closet in a couple of months. Otherwise, invest in your wardrobe just as you would a stock portfolio—look for pieces that will continue to keep their value or even appreciate over the years—and that you will continue to appreciate.

There is nothing like a person who wears clothes with confidence, poise, and flair. Whether you are Nicole Kidman, Anna Wintour, or the manager of the local bank, knowing how to wear what you have and how to choose what to wear is an important component of the formula for success!

## 5. *Plastic Surgery*

I don't know what this says about the times in which we live, but in this era of Botox injections and extreme makeovers, of trimming toes (not toenails, toes!) so that they'll look better in shoes, I would be remiss in not covering plastic surgery as an option for getting the look you want.

There are responsible plastic surgeons out there who will, for example, not give my aunt in Cincinnati a face-lift until she quits smoking, or up-and-coming New York plastic surgeon Dr. Phillip Miller, who won't take on a client until he or she first addresses a questionnaire about their nutritional habits, their exercise regimen, and what they hope to achieve via their surgery (if they purposely want to look like a cat or to model themselves after Brad Pitt, he won't take them on). Dr. Miller knows that while outward appearance is important, it's just one element of how we feel about ourselves, and of how others see us.

There are plenty of plastic-surgery cautionary tales, from Melanie Griffith to Courtney Love to Jennifer

Grey—the *Dirty Dancing* star who made the unfortunate mistake of listening to people who told her that to re-jumpstart her career she should get herself a smaller nose. Now she just looks like everyone else, and as far as I can tell, her career is not exactly on fire.

But then again there's the story of Pamela Anderson, whose career has been boosted by her breast implants (she is, after all, known for her Barbie-doll body). There are probably thousands of stories out there like that, though if the actor or actress has a fantastic PR person who can permanently hide the "before" pictures, we may never know for sure. . . .

I certainly don't condemn those who want to go out and have their skin repaved, the lines between their eyes Botoxed, their stomachs stapled, their earlobes delicately trimmed, their brows lifted. But I have to say I vastly prefer the cast of the late, great *Sex and the City*, especially Sarah Jessica Parker, who went from being a *Square Pegs* geek to a fashion icon with the help of stylists, makeup artists, hair specialists, Patricia Field, and her own quirky and inventive sense of confidence. Not with a doctor's scalpel.

Or take someone like Adrian Brody, Oscar-winning star of *The Pianist*, who effectively plays up what some might consider his biggest detriment—his huge nose. The nose didn't seem to get in the way of his excellent Oscar smooch with Halle Berry, for all the world to see!

So if you do decide to go under the knife, first think about all the cautionary tales, especially Michael Jackson and Faye Dunaway. If you are okay with those images and still want to proceed, do your homework. Thoroughly check out your doctor and anesthesiologist. You don't want to end up like Olivia Goldsmith, the author of *The First Wives' Club*, who died on the table having her chin and neck done. I probably don't need to say much more than "Joan Rivers" in order for you to know what I mean.

The primary message of this chapter is to appreciate what God gave you, and make the most of it. Now, go out there, and DAZZLE!

---

Helpful plastic surgery Web sites: Beth Landman, a contributing editor to *New York* magazine who specializes in beauty and plastic surgery, says: "Check out your doctor on the board of health Web site; if more than two people have complained about your doctor, it will be listed. You always want to make sure the doctor is board certified and know there is a difference between facial plastic surgeon doctors and other plastic surgery experts. Facial plastic surgeons would not be board certified as plastic surgeons—they are certified ear, nose, and throat doctors. Another good way to check up on a doctor is to see if he or she is a member of the Aesthetic Society. The top doctors are all certified by the American Society for Plastic Surgery and are all listed on the group's Web site." The Aesthetic Society's number is 847-228-9900.

## Chapter Five

# Get Yourself Good PR, or The Art of the Campaign

P UBLICIST: (PƏ-BLƏ-SIST) N. ONE WHO RELENTLESSLY stalks me and my colleagues to get coverage for his or her clients. Otherwise known as the devil's spawn, gatekeepers, masters of manipulation, gods and goddesses (when they are able to get me that quote by deadline time), banes of my existence, and necessary evils.

---

PR dressing: Part of a good PR person's job is to "dress" their clients, either by calling a designer themselves or hiring a stylist to do it. If an A-list star is wearing a designer's frock, both the star and designer win. The star looks good and the frock maker gets press. Dressing stars is BIG business. Many people have gotten fired from places like Prada, Calvin Klein, Versace, Valentino, etc., because they could not get a celebrity to wear their clothes to the big events like the Oscars, Golden Globes, or MTV Music Awards. I will never forget the 2003 Golden Globes. I was trying to console an inconsolable publicist who worked for a big name designer and could not find anyone to dress. She was worried about her job. She should have been—that's all her job was: to get celebs to wear the designer's clothes!

Chances are that if there is a big star wearing Harry Winston diamonds and a Dior dress while walking the red carpet, the woman she's holding hands with is her publicist. Don't think, when the cover of the new *Vanity Fair* features a photo of a comely young actor or actress you've barely—if ever—heard of, that that cover came into being just because some enterprising *Vanity Fair* editor said, "Hmm. I like that rising young star and have a hunch they'd make a great cover for us!" That would be as naïve as believing that a star could be born sitting at the soda counter at Schwab's. In the world of entertainment, very little happens in terms of media coverage that a publicist isn't in some way involved with.

The big PR agencies who represent the top stars in the business play one client off another. Want an interview with Tom Cruise? Okay, then take an interview with Ms. Nobody, too. You want me to get you an exclusive sit-down with Harrison Ford (a star, by the way, who almost never does interviews) . . . well first you're going to have to put Kate Hudson on the cover of the magazine. "It happened organically" is not a phrase that is very often applied to the way big stars achieve celebrity. Yes, it's true that most of the big stars have a certain something, or a combination of somethings, that keeps them on the top. But getting there? Believe me, it wasn't an accident.

PR, otherwise known as public relations or press relations, is big business. It controls how film studios, TV networks, movie and television stars, musicians, authors, and even corporations and politicians interact with the media and the public. The images that you get are largely prepared by PR people, and then interpreted by those of us who work for newspapers, magazines, TV, radio, and, increasingly, Web sites. Do I take whatever a publicist feeds me and swallow it hook, line, and sinker? Rarely, and only if I know and trust the person.

Am I able to differentiate a publicist who knows what I need, whom I can trust, from someone who will do or say anything to get their client a plug, without regard for me or my position? Hell, yeah. How can I tell the difference? Instincts, honed via hard experience.

My favorite items are always the ones I dig up myself, witness with my own eyes, get from the horse's mouth, rather than from the horse's publicist. Still, there is no denying that publicists have been behind many of the best showbiz stories of the times (either helping to create them in the first place, or letting reporters like me in on them), and that they are invaluable sources of information not only about their own clients, but—if they're good—also about the industry as a whole.

PR is basically all about marketing. In the case of a movie actor or actress, it may be about getting people to pay attention to the movie, or to the performance, but it's also about pushing a commodity, a brand, so that next time around, audiences will say: "Oh, it's an Olsen twins movie. I want to see it." Or, "It's an Angelina Jolie film. I have to go." Or "It's a Coen Brothers picture, and I've seen every one since *Raising Arizona*."

Marketing also works with product placement, such as when Nokia paid millions of dollars to have its phones featured in the movie *Charlie's Angels*. Great marketing can make people say, "I need some lip balm, everyone uses Carmex," Or "Earl Jeans are the *best*!" You get the picture.

The sitcom *Friends* is another example. The cast was really onto something when they decided to stick together, both on and off the set. They promoted the show via DVDs, books, and other merchandise. They made it so that *Friends* was not just a television show, it was a cultural phenomenon that was pretty much impossible to avoid.

One can see this today in just about any business. Look at Starbucks, or Target's hiring of "cool" designers such as Isaac Mizrahi and Cynthia Rowley. Or the way the latest hip cell phone to carry changes from a Nokia to a Motorola, and so on, depending on who's carrying a particular brand of phone. (And if you think that most of the celebrities brandishing that phone aren't getting it for free from the company as a way of establishing the brand as a must-have, I have a bridge I can sell you.) This sort of "brand" promotion is widely used now—Lizzie Grubman was onto it from the very earliest days, at one point pronouncing traditional PR "dead." Whether it's Martha Stewart, Victoria's Secret, Newman's Own, or HBO, branding is huge.

How does all of this apply to you if you want to build your business, build yourself as a brand? How do you take the rules of big-time PR and make them work for you?

---

Karma can be a bitch, but it can also take you to the head of the line. People will be wholeheartedly interested in you and gladly support you if you treat them well. It will also cushion your fall if you stumble along the way.

---

In the immortal words of our good friend Couri Hay, in its simplest form, PR is "good word of mouth. It's having your friends speak well of you, having your teachers speak well of you, your family . . . Then maybe your hometown newspaper notices you because you're just the best cheerleader, or the best quarterback—good PR usually comes from doing something well, being the best at something." So, if you do something well for someone, he or she will tell his or her friends, and the word will be passed on.

Or sometimes it just comes from doing a great job publicizing something!

What is the best thing you can do for yourself in terms of creating a buzz, getting media coverage for yourself or your business or your product—getting good PR? Couri explains, "Whether it's basketball or softball—or baking the best brownie or creating the best prom decorations or raising money for the opera or the symphony—concentrate on what you're doing and do it well, then worry about whether Page Six or Liz Smith or your local society editor is noticing you."

Steven Gaines, editor of ihamptons.com, observes simply, "Publicity is key to success." After doing something really well and becoming the master of your trade, you need to be a good salesman! If you just don't have it in you to hawk yourself or your products and you can afford it, hire an expert to do it for you.

A good PR person understands that publicity is a two-way street. Not only do you have to want it, people have to want to hear it. People want to believe certain urban legends and fairy tales about how big stars got "discovered" because it's very "American" to imagine that the American dream applies to Hollywood. The biggest Hollywood myth is "Oh, I was walking down the street and Steven Spielberg stopped me and said, 'You'd be perfect for . . .' and then he puts me in his movie." That's not how it happens, that's how they say it happens. People love those types of stories, and they eat them up. They want to think they could take two weeks in L.A. and Tom Cruise is going to put them in his next film because they rode the bus together. It doesn't happen like that. And not only because Tom Cruise isn't riding too many buses anymore!

An example of how much lengthy, behind-the-scenes masterminding goes into the "making" of an overnight success can be found in the case of celebrity magician David Blaine. PR maven Dan Klores was first introduced to Blaine in talent agent Johnny Podell's office at ICM in New York. Blaine had prepared a videotape in black-and-white of himself on the streets of New York City doing magic tricks. The majority of his tricks were card tricks, but some "mentalism" was involved. Every time he read someone's mind or picked the right card from their hand, the crowd would go wild, oohing and aahing, demanding to be next. Blaine then turns to Klores (who by the way has seen it all and rarely falls for new talent) and impresses him further with a series of perfectly performed card tricks. Klores realizes Blaine is the real deal, and so comes up with a plan to bring Blaine to the public, and makes him huge.

The first order of business? Package him. Give him a story: "You're half Puerto Rican, half Jewish. You're this genius," he told him. Klores then went about thinking of how he could play into Blaine's ethnic background with audiences and sell him as a Puerto Rican Jew. Next? Get him known. So he brings him to the office of Kurt Andersen, who at the time was editor of the ever-influential *New York* magazine. Klores recalls that it was a Friday evening, and a group of editors and writers were assembled in the room. He had told them that he was bringing someone amazing named David Blaine, but didn't tell them anything else about him ahead of time. (They trusted Dan, because he already had established credibility with the press.) Blaine performed a series of tricks for the assembled group. "They were blown away," according to Klores. The result? The first feature on David Blaine appeared in *New York* magazine. This was soon followed by write-ups in the *New York Post* and *Daily News*, and in countless other venues. Jimmy Nederlander took notice and started to bankroll and manage Blaine's career.

Blaine himself was a quick publicity study and took it upon himself to forge relationships with stars like Leonardo DiCaprio, which made for great publicity. He also got himself quoted in the press for questioning David Copperfield's abilities as a magician. He definitely knew how to work it.

Shortly after slagging off Copperfield in print, Blaine started orchestrating big stunts, such as spending two days packed in ice in Times Square, wearing only a pair of shorts. The stunt itself may not exactly have been the most dramatic or exciting (the only excitement, in truth, came when Blaine's girlfriend tripped over his catheter), but it worked to get his name in the papers and his image on TV.

And that is how david blaine became DAVID BLAINE.

Another PR success story? Aimster.com. In the beginning, Aimster was just another file-sharing Web site, debuting alongside countless others. Matthew Rich says that to make the music-sharing site stand out from the pack, he fell back on that most time-tested, surefire rule of sales: sex sells. The founder had a daughter named Amy whom the site was named after, and, Rich recalls, "We advertised her as the co-creator of the Web site, and billed her as 'the Aimster girl.' We did a makeover . . . made her very sexy. We went about as far as I felt was responsible to go on a sixteen-year-old, even though the father said, 'Go farther, go farther.' I started getting her out to parties, getting her photographed with Heath Ledger at the premiere of *A Knight's Tale*. She was at Gorbachev's seventieth birthday party, and he said, 'Oh, my granddaughter knows your site!' We put pictures of him on the Web site with her. . . . She was so hot!"

Rich recalls that at the time Napster was taking a lot of heat from the record industry over copyright infringement, and so Aimster was positioned along the lines of the good Napster (not for people who were slackers looking to rip off the recording industry), complete with the Aimster angel. Features in newspapers all over the country followed, and the mission was complete. (In the interests of full disclosure, Aimster later did go out of business, but thanks to great PR, it had its day in the sun!)

What's the moral of the story? Once you have your "product," figure out how to sell it and use every opportunity you can to spread the word. Be creative. Don't be afraid to use your connections. Dedicate yourself to the cause!

It's also essential to educate yourself about your own hometown. In order to be at the right place at the right time, you have to be able to get in the door.

It's all about the listings section in your local paper. You know, that awfully boring section in the back that makes your head swim, which has lots of tiny events and movie and restaurant listings. That section can be the key to your success, as it has the openings and lifelines you are looking for.

Dina Wise, the head of events for Miramax Films, offers sage advice about becoming known in all the right places. Say you want to start getting seen in the hot clubs or restaurants, but you might not feel you can get in on your own steam. During off hours, maybe earlier in the evening or at the end of the night, go and introduce yourself to the doormen, the bouncers, the maitre d's; get to know them. Then enjoy it as people gape when you are ushered right in.

In Los Angeles, according to MTV producer Jillian Kogan, "People know the way to get into all the parties—all the Motorola parties, all the magazine launch parties, the *Vanity Fair* party at the Oscars, whatever it is. They gotta know the publicists, because they control the lists."

If you don't have a lot of connections and you are living in a big city like New York, Los Angeles,

Chicago, etc., do your homework. If you see a party listed in the newspaper, find out whether there's a publicity firm handling it, and call them to see if you can exchange favors with them to get in. Now, I don't mean sexual favors. What I mean is, everyone needs something to help them out in their lives. Perhaps you work in a law firm—maybe they need some legal advice? Or you run a florist shop, and everyone always needs flowers at a party or in their office. . . .

If you live in a small town, befriend the newspaper's calendar or society editor, and see if he or she will give you a heads-up regarding events that might provide you with a networking venue. Washington, D.C., is a big city, but in many ways it is a small town, at least when it comes to social networks. Find out who the big PR firms are and who their clients are. If, say, you are opening a bakery in Georgetown, offer to donate some of your baked goods at the next big event being thrown in exchange for being able to attend and hand out your card. If you are a clothing designer just launching a new line, find out who does fashion PR. If you can't hire them yet yourself, see if there's a way that, in exchange for providing them with some free pieces from your line, they can get you press coverage.

How to be your own best publicist:

1) Always—and always, I mean every single time you leave the house—put your best foot forward and act appropriately.
2) Set time aside every day for marketing you and your company. This will most likely double your work load, but it is worth it.
3) Take the time to research all the appropriate editors, reporters, and freelance writers who "cover" your specific area.
4) Make up your own marketing package, complete with a photo of you and your product, information on your company, and press clippings, if you have any.
5) Come up with your own storyline and sell it.
6) Memorize the next chapter, on press.

This is a principle that can work anywhere. In Maplewood, New Jersey, the owner of a cybercafe, NetNomads, knows from her prior experience on Wall Street that you've got to give a little to get a little. When the local middle school is looking for a place to print its monthly newsletter, for example, she offers to do it for a significantly discounted price in the hope that her name will get out there, and that in the future, others will come to her because they've heard she is great to do business with. Or if you want to be the next Mrs. Fields, with your own national line of cookies, bake a great batch and send them out to all the local media (in proper packaging, please. These days, if anyone is sent anything in a pie plate with Reynolds Wrap covering it, it goes straight in the trash.). Offer to provide dessert for a local charity—anything, so people will start eating, talking, and ultimately, buying.

Which brings us to the next rule of thumb: Cultivate relationships!

Hollis Gillespie is currently a humor writer for *Creative Loafing* in Atlanta. Not too long ago, she was a flight attendant who only dreamed of being a humor writer, but when she met Atlanta PR wiz Liz Lapidis, Liz became the ace up her sleeve. According to Liz, "After September 11, Hollis came into my office, plopped down and said: 'I don't want to fly anymore—you gotta help me.'" Liz was intrigued by the challenge, put her in touch with a contact at National Public Radio, and gave her a few other names of people who might be interested in her writing. It didn't take too long before she ended up on NPR. An editor at a publishing house heard the piece and loved it. He offered her a two-book deal worth six figures and she was on her way. Where would we be without our friends?

---

Paparazzi are your pals: There have been countless times when I have seen freelance photographers act as PR for people they like. They will take photos (usually of a beautiful woman) and exhort the photo editors they work with to use them—and it works! This is how Lola Pagnani had her moment of fame in New York back in 2001. A D-list nude model and sometime actress in her homeland of Italy, Pagnani had been to New York before, trying to break into the "scene." But she got lucky in the summer of 2000 when she befriended Aubrey Reuben, a high school principal-turned-celebrity photographer who has a penchant for the theater (and, as it turns out, for nude girls). Lola, unnaturally endowed with double-F breasts and a nonexistent nose, was photographed by Reuben at a party. The two became romantically involved, and Reuben dutifully campaigned for Lola to get featured in the *New York Post*. He succeeded, and soon after that, for over three months, darling Lola was in every paper in Manhattan and received over a dozen calls from Hollywood producers eager to offer her roles. But before Lola could take advantage of her big break, she made her crucial mistake: She cut off her ties with Reuben to hang out with a *New York Times* writer, who stopped being her friend within a month after writing one article about her. Lola burned her bridges, and sadly, her "It"-dom dissipated almost as quickly as it arose.

---

Or take what PR guru Lizzie Grubman did for actress Tara Reid . . .

Up until 1998, Tara Reid's biggest claim to fame was one line in the Coen Brothers' film *The Big Lebowski*. Prior to that, there had been years of walk-on appearances on D-list soap operas and the mystifyingly long-running after-school sitcom *Head of the Class*. A close pal of Lizzie's introduced Tara and Lizzie and credits Lizzie with whatever success Tara ultimately achieved. She recalls, "Lizzie used to take Tara out to all of her parties and yell out, 'Oh my God! That's the girl from *The Big Lebowski*!' or just go up to photographers and tell them to take Tara's picture because she was 'in *The Big Lebowski* and was going to be HUGE!'" Grubman then browbeat photographers and photo editors at the major New York papers into using the shots of Tara. It might not have been the most sophisticated publicity campaign, but it worked! (Tara later dumped Lizzie and hired another big PR firm, which is probably why she's having so many problems right now.)

A trick Lizzie is adept at is one you can use yourself. Bend over backwards to do favors for people, because then someone will always owe you a favor.

Here's an example of how it works: Publicist A knows the talent booker at the *Good Morning America* show. Diane Sawyer really wants Publicist A's top-billed talent, and the booker calls Publicist A, who makes it happen. Two months later, Publicist A's lesser-known client, a struggling singer, desperately needs to get some press, so Publicist A calls in her favor and *voila!* Miraculously, Diane Sawyer is interviewing the struggling singer on the show.

So much of PR is about connections. Take the case of Matthew McConaughey.

In 1994, Matthew McConaughey was looking at obscurity, up close. The vaguely talented, hunky young actor had scored several forgettable roles and had once even gotten lucky, managing to snag a part in Richard Linklater's cult classic, *Dazed and Confused*. Still, the "big time" eluded him.

But about a year later, he managed to catch the eye of PR powerhouse Pat Kingsley, often described as the dragon lady of publicity. Standing at an imposing 5 feet, 11 inches, Kingsley is a permanent fixture at every film premiere and awards ceremony, tirelessly herding her stars between journalists and fans, personally deciding who gets access and who doesn't. Pat became one of the most powerful women in Hollywood by refining the art of press control. She gathered a list of powerful clients and through intimidation or "blackouts," i.e., refusing certain reporters or publications access to her clients because of negative pieces they had previously done, she totally controlled media access to her roster, which included Jodie Foster and Al Pacino. (She was widely credited with building Tom Cruise into the powerhouse he is today, but he left her in 2004 to have his sister, LeeAnn Devett, a fellow Scientologist, help drive his career.) You always pick up the phone when Pat Kingsley calls, and you never want to piss her off.

"I met Matthew through his manager at the time," Pat said. "I don't remember the woman's name, but at the time we worked with other clients of hers as well." Not that Matthew was an easy client. In the beginning he didn't understand that PR was important. "I had to chase Matthew," Pat laughed. While some in Hollywood credit Pat with using her contacts to score him auditions, which eventually landed him his big breakout role in *A Time to Kill*, Pat denies this. "That wasn't my job," she said.

But getting Matthew press and attention, as a new actor, *was* her job—and she did it very well. In mid-1996, before he had even appeared in a leading role, she got him the cover of *Vanity Fair*. This was a real gamble on the part of *Vanity Fair* editor Graydon Carter, since McConaughey was a nobody at the time. Following that came other magazine covers and countless other interviews and features. Some might argue that his acting talent is limited, but there's no question that today Matthew is considered a highly bankable star. That is the power of PR done right.

The story of Molly Sims, former nobody, is also instructive. In 1998 she was just another Wonderbra model with a great rack and a dazzling smile. But then she met Lewis Kay, a PR exec at Bragman Nyman Cafarelli. Soon, Lewis was also enlisted to do some PR work for his new friend. Molly is smart about such things. She knows the first two rules of modeling: 1) If you don't marry rich you are screwed; 2) Your career will be over by age thirty. Molly knew that no amount of Botox would sufficiently turn back the clock once she hit a certain age, so she'd have to start branching out.

Soon after the two got together, another client of Lewis's, Rebecca Romijn-Stamos, decided she wanted to quit her gig as host of MTV's *House of Style* and pursue an acting career. I bet you can guess what happened next—Molly got the MTV job, thanks to Lewis's contacts and influence. She instantly became a hit, and three years and one *Sports Illustrated* swimsuit cover later, Molly had made such a name for herself that she could now headline an event, and was always bombarded by photographers. Sadly, Lewis dropped Molly when he felt fame went to her head and she became too demanding, and without Lewis's guidance, her career seems to have faltered.

Many a career has been made (or broken, for that matter) by staging a well-timed, well-conceived publicity stunt. (Does anybody out there remember Tiny Tim tiptoeing through the tulips?) The stunt can be something like David Blaine's bizarre and masochistic displays, or something quirkier—local, along the lines of something Atlanta PR maven Liz Lapidis staged for one of her clients, a cheesemaker. "We once did a stunt that was really funny," she told me.

"Our client arranges a nightly cheese course at Woodfire Grill. So for April Fool's we sent out a press release 'Woodfire Grill Cuts the Cheese: exploring the art of processed cheese, served with wine by the glass. For more information contact Jenny Jenny at 867–5309.'" You know, the phone number in that Eighties song? Lapidis says, "It got picked up by all the little gossip columns—it was just funny and one of those insider buzz things. Sometimes that's the best stuff."

Believe it or not, a lot of Hollywood publicity stunts come in the form of fake items about romantic relationships that don't really exist. Some PR people fall back on this to get their client attention. Ever notice that every time Penelope Cruz is in a movie there is "news" that she is dating her co-star? It happened with Nicolas Cage and *Captain Corelli's Mandolin*—thus buzz was generated for an otherwise horrific movie that basically bombed. Next she "dated" Matt Damon, her *All the Pretty Horses* co-star, at least until she finally did hook up with Tom Cruise for *Vanilla Sky*. At the time of this writing, she is with her *Sahara* co-star Matthew McConaughey. Hmm.

Jennifer Lopez (or her handlers) also has been known to play the faux relationship game, a trick borrowed from the Hollywood of past eras. In early

2002, when she was still married to dancer Chris Judd (however briefly), she began a "fling" with Ben Affleck. The fling worked two ways—to get her out of her six-month marriage (she was said to have paid Judd upwards of $15 million to set her free) and to publicize the two movies she was making with Affleck, those unforgettable pieces of celluloid history, *Gigli* and *Jersey Girl*. However, in between these she also made a movie with Ralph Fiennes, *Maid in Manhattan*. Wouldn't you know it? I got a call from someone involved in that film telling me she and Fiennes were "canoodling." A day later, paparazzi snapped the two together hugging and kissing, after a well-timed phone tip. Or rather, they caught Lopez hugging and kissing Fiennes, who looked distinctly uncomfortable, since he was involved in a long-term, committed relationship with Francesca Annis. Within days, Lopez was "back" with Affleck. Fiennes was so annoyed by the whole episode that he refused to go to the premiere, and even went on record saying the leak of the alleged fling was "not organic." To my knowledge he has yet to speak to Lopez again.

Meanwhile, just days later, on Lopez's thirty-fourth birthday, Page Six received a call from her camp alerting us to a "photo op." We were told Lopez, her sister, her mother, and some close friends would be dining at the tony New York restaurant The Park, celebrating along with Affleck. For all to see, Affleck gave Lopez a $200,000 diamond bracelet and a long kiss, recorded for posterity by the attending photographers. When *People* magazine gave a lot of space to the "spontaneous" event, lots of readers suspected the incident of being staged, and said as much in letters they sent in. Well, turns out maybe that one wasn't a publicity stunt. Still, Lopez definitely milked it for what it was worth, and then some!

---

The Fame Sandwich: When two B-listers make an A-lister: Sometimes when two not-so-famous stars hook up, they create a force that propels them both ahead. As my colleague Chris Wilson says, "When two stars get together, it's not an addition of fame, it's a multiplication of fame." Look at Ashton and Demi, Brad and Jen, the former Bennifer (Ben and Jen), Jessica Simpson and Nick Lachey . . . you get the point. Sometimes an alliance can make you much, much stronger.

---

PR stunts can work to put someone on the map or even to deflect controversy. Take the case of Michael Jackson and all the pictures that got taken of him with Brooke Shields, nicely timed to offset questions like "Why doesn't Michael have a girlfriend?" which surfaced right around the time he started getting accused of molesting young boys. The possibility that the couple was engaged began to circulate in the press, and they were witnessed nuzzling at several high-profile events. Several years after their much-publicized "breakup," Brooke publicly acknowledged that she and Michael had never been intimate, much less tongue-kissed. Most of us weren't all that surprised.

A few years later, in 1993, just several months after his reported $20 million payoff to a young boy, Michael once again became linked to a bona fide woman, this time to Elvis Presley's Scientologist daughter, Lisa Marie. Then there was the "kiss" stunt—when Michael and Lisa Marie announced their coupledom and quickie marriage at the 1994 Grammy Awards, and sealed it with a rather awkward, messy, even freakish kiss. The audience was stunned, but no one save Michael's most ardent fans (and trust me, there are more than a few) believed the scene was authentic. About a year later, the two divorced.

Oddly enough, sometimes the exact opposite happens, and two people who really are a couple need to pretend they're not. In 1999, that was the case with Britney and Justin, who were at the height of their popularity. They had secretly been dating for three years, having met when they were preteens performing in the Mickey Mouse Club. They fell in love just as their careers were taking off. However, to preserve their innocent virginal images, and to stay single and therefore "available" in the eyes of their fans, they kept it hush-hush. One PR person with knowledge of the situation told me that "all of a sudden these rumors of them being together started circulating. It was horrible—their fans were going nuts, they didn't like it at all. Especially when those teenybopper boybands start out, their fans like to at least dream they have a chance with them." So Britney's PR team put their heads together and came up with a solution. "We hired a Justin Timberlake look-alike to escort Britney everywhere," the PR person told me. "When she would go to a premiere or something, she was with this two-bit actor and we would look at the press and say, 'See, we told you she's not with Justin, she's with someone who LOOKS like Justin!' They bought it hook, line, and sinker." At least for a while. In 2001, the pair admitted they really were an item, and then in 2002, they broke up.

Take also the case of Jessica Simpson and Nick Lachey. In the spring of 2001, their respective careers had fallen on hard times. They'd had their moment in the sun, but now it was cloud time. Then, suddenly, the golden couple broke up. The breakup of the sweet virgin and her patient boyfriend garnered them lots of publicity. Then the two "reunited" right after September 11, saying the disastrous event made them realize they were meant for each other. Several months later, it was suggested the breakup had been a publicity stunt.

And what about those who use mental breakdowns or health scares to generate ink? The old "I'm going into rehab so give me some sympathy—and a story in *People*," or "I had a stomach bypass, so give me the cover of *Us*" has, at least temporarily, revived more than one flagging career. Tacky, but true!

---

Damage control code words: Sometimes, when a star is in trouble and reporters get a whiff that something is not right, PR people will try to stave them off with "PR Speak." Here, to help you decode what they say, are my translations of terms that ALWAYS mean something else.

"So-and-so has food poisoning." Translation: drug overdose. Other drug overdose terms are dehydration, strained throat (for singers), and any minor or common illness (as in a cold, the flu, etc).

"So-and-so just needs some rest." Translation: mental breakdown. Other breakdown terms are stress and exhaustion.

When an actor or singer wants to break their contract by either not doing a movie or a tour, they will commonly cite "previous obligations." Or they may suddenly develop an injury, as Tobey Maguire was accused of. The story goes back when Tobey was filming *Seabiscuit,* he decided he wanted more money for *Spider-Man 2.* He told Sony Studios he had injured his back on *Seabiscuit*, and if they didn't cough up more dough, he wouldn't be un-injured in time. Sony told him to go away, and they tried to hire Jake Gyllenhaal . . . until Tobey realized his mistake and used the influence of his powerful agents to help him get back into *Spider-Man*—with the raise he desired. Some people in Hollywood snarked the back injury was a ruse to make a higher salary but indeed Tobey's back was hurt. To quote Ralph Fiennes, I'm sure he thinks the raise was "organic."

---

Of course there's also a tradition of more risqué publicity stunts—for example, there's the man who attended classes at Stanford University naked. He was swiftly dubbed "Naked Man" and offered spots on talk shows, interviewed for newspapers and magazines, and the like, all because he hated to wear clothing (or so he said).

Another example: In 1995 Altoids were all but obsolete. Its owner, Kraft, a "family" company, hired the PR firm Rogers & Cowan to cook up something to jumpstart the mint brand. What did they come up with? Let's put it this way: Soon thereafter, *Cosmopolitan* ran a cover story titled something like "How to Give Your Man a Better Blow Job with Altoids." Kraft naturally denied they'd had anything to do with starting this new trend, which has caught on everywhere! But no doubt Kraft—and Rogers & Cowan—are laughing all the way to the bank! You might say the stunt blew life into a limp brand. . . .

But beware of publicity stunts—they can backfire.

Witness George Michael, the now washed-up British pop pervert. In 2002, his career had waned when Michael produced a new song called "Walking the Dog," which poked fun at President George Bush, British Prime Minister Tony Blair, and portrayed Americans as maniacal gun nuts. He continued his America-bashing in all of his media interviews, and Americans responded by not buying his record. There's a lesson in this: Never insult the people you are trying to woo!

Another stunt that backfired (not to pick on Michael Jackson, but let's face it, it's hard not to!) was when Jackson called a press conference and boarded a double-decker bus holding a sign that read TOMMY MOTTOLA IS THE DEVIL. Mottola, at the time, was the head of Sony Records, which owns Michael's label, Epic. Michael, apparently forgetting that the American public had come to associate him more with alleged child molesting than with his music, chose to blame Tommy for the miserable sales of his $60 million album, ironically titled *Invincible*.

During the press conference, Michael accused Tommy of being a racist and began blathering about how the music industry is biased against black artists. Several problems with this argument: 1) Michael had never appeared to care about any of this before, at least not until his career seemed to be fading; 2) Michael has spent his entire life trying to be white; and 3) this battle was already being undertaken by black and white artists who had teamed up to fight racism, including Courtney Love, the Dixie Chicks, and others. 4) Tommy was once married to Mariah Carey, who is biracial. 5) Tommy has promoted and founded the careers of many artists of all races. Hello, Michael!!

His move backfired. The press picked up on how Jackson, who had always seemed to have an endless supply of cash, was now broke and trying to get out of paying the $200 million he owed Sony. Jackson learned the hard way he shouldn't bite the hand that feeds him, not to mention that people are now afraid to work with him, feeling that if he turned on Tommy, someday he would also turn on them.

In my experience, you always get more flies with honey. So go on the attack only when absolutely necessary!

If you decide that it is time to hire your own publicist, make sure you are hiring someone who is not only effective but also a kindred spirit. Dina Wise puts it this way: "Find someone with a personality that mirrors your own." She observes that your PR person will have to be your spokesperson at times, "will have to anticipate your every move and most of all, they will have to want you to be famous as much as you do."

---

Five questions to ask a PR person before hiring them:

1) What kinds of clients do you have?
2) What is your main area of expertise?
3) What can you do for me specifically?
4) What would you do if, God forbid, something really bad should happen and I was arrested?
5) Here are my goals for the next five years. How can you help me achieve them? And how can you help brand me, personally?

---

There are many times, I've observed, when a PR person can't get hold of their client right away, and therefore will have to use their own judgment, speaking on behalf of the client. If you've hired a publicist who has no real idea what makes you tick, what you're about, this can be a recipe for disaster. Say a gossip columnist has called to say that you have been caught *in flagrante* at the local Motel 6 with three members of a boy-band. Your PR person, who doesn't really know you all that well and can't find you to respond, answers, "Well, she is free, heterosexual, and twenty-one." (This may sound incredible but in my time at Page Six, I have heard similar lines uttered to me. I am not kidding.) Only problem is, you're a devout Christian fundamentalist, and not only do you not want your parents thinking this is true, your fans will be outraged if they think it is. It would be far more constructive had your publicist answered, "That's impossible, as my client was at Bible study that evening." Only he or she never would have thought of it, because you barely know each other!

There's another reason you will want a PR person you are simpatico with: There are a lot of incredibly annoying publicists out there. Do you really want to hire one who will drive you (and the media) around the bend?

Don't be afraid to hire a PR person who is shameless!

Over a decade ago, Denise Rich had ditched her no-good billionaire hubby, Marc Rich, and was looking for something to do with the billions she'd received in the divorce settlement, when she found her calling: writing schlocky songs. Enter Bobby Zarem, the portly, flamboyant PR legend who takes credit for inventing the I Love New York campaign in the Seventies (note: This is a widely disputed claim, especially by the ad agency which also claims to have come up with it.). A never-married native of South Carolina, Bobby is an old school publicist. In contrast to the newer crop of PR folk, Zarem talks a lot, has epic feuds which often seem to overshadow the publicity he generates for his clientele, and treats his employees like slaves. (One employee hated him so much he regularly gave his boss Zarem, a diabetic, coffee with sugar in it in the hopes it would kill him.) Despite all of this, he was still a very effective publicist.

The height of Zarem's power was during the Seventies, Eighties, and early Nineties, when he handled premieres for most of the major movie studios, was on a speed-dial basis with all of the studio heads, and had most newspaper columnists by the short and curlies. Within a year of his working with Denise Rich, she began to be considered a "well known" songwriter and a charity-circuit powerhouse. How did he do it? By harassing his media contacts, of course.

Trust me, you don't know harassment until you have Bobby Zarem on your tail. He will call and fax incessantly, begging, pleading, even crying, until you agree to put something in the paper about his client. Since Bobby knows everyone at every paper, Denise was a "successful songwriter" within a year, or at least she was as far as newspaper readers were concerned, which was apparently enough to prompt music companies to start calling her.

In 2001, Denise faced some serious PR damage-control issues, after she helped her ex-hubby get a pardon from Bill Clinton. At that point she dropped Bobby and hired Howard Rubenstein to guide her through.

Bobby's star has faded since his heyday, and these days he is semi-retired, though he does muster the energy every now and then to help a young, struggling star.

Joe Duer was one such beneficiary. The hot young model was trying to break into acting when he hooked up with Bobby a few years ago. At the time, unfortunately, Bobby had a gangrenous infection in his foot, and was hobbling around on crutches and in a cast, though he managed to take his protégé Joe to several parties a week. He introduced him to the James Bond producer Barbara Broccolli at one such event, and got him a part as the hunky UPS delivery man who gets to ogle a scantily clad Cameron Diaz in *Charlie's Angels*. I admit that Page Six ran something on Joe—what choice did we have, with Bobby calling all the time?

---

Okay, okay. In the interest of full disclosure and total honesty, Joe Duer has actually made it into Page Six several times. We are not proud.

---

There have been many cases of people who have used family members or non-professional PR people to get the job done. Take Kathy Hilton, proud mother of the Hilton hotel heirs, Paris and Nicky. She refers to her daughters as "the family business," which is also how she treats them.

For years, before the girls were "legal" in any respect, Kathy worked to get her gangly daughters invited to all the right parties—one time, on the day of the Golden Globes party in 2002, calling thirty-five times in one day to gain her underage girls entry into the soiree. This was of course prior to Paris's infamous sexcapades, and before the debut of her show on Fox. Back in 2002, Paris and Nicky were just two very young, pretty, rich girls who seemed to be everywhere. But Kathy always refused to take no for an answer, and managed to introduce the girls to everyone. She was also known to take gossip columnists out for dinner when they started getting a little catty about her product, I mean, her daughters. To some, the girls' antics—dressing like hookers, dancing on tables while wearing no underwear, getting drunk and vomiting in public, making home videos—might be considered appalling, but to their proud mother, this looked like what she would consider brilliant brand extension. I should note that her persistence paid off long before the start of *The Simple Life*. By that time the girls had already appeared on the cover of the popular men's magazine *FHM*, been featured in *Vanity Fair*, the London society rag *Tatler*, and were a regular staple of gossip columns. Then in July 2002, Paris signed with talent agency UTA and with the Ford Modeling Agency. She also scored a role in *Zoolander*. That and, of course, *The Simple Life*. Bobby Zarem couldn't have done better than dear old Mom!

There are plenty of other celebrities out there who have been managed by their mothers, or who at least have strong-willed "stage" mothers, including Brandy, Brittany Murphy, Melissa Joan Hart, and Sarah Michelle Gellar.

Believe it or not, Harrison Ford is one of the few major stars who's never had a PR person. He prefers to direct press to his manager, Pat McQueeney. Sean

Connery and Robert Redford also count on their managers or agents when it comes to press strategy, but then again, it's not exactly as if these guys need someone to get them more press!

WARNING: Most of us out there don't have to worry about overexposure—after all, you are just starting out and want all the press you can get. But there is a fine line, and sometimes even an experienced publicist will take her client over that line.

Back to Matthew McConaughey, who after that year of magazine covers, interviews, film roles, etc., seemed to be everywhere—you couldn't get away from him. Now I like pistachio ice cream, but if you gave me a gallon of it every day, I'd get sick of it. And that's what happened with McConaughey. After his huge launch, he flopped. PR was blamed for overexposing him. Today he is repped by Alan Nierob, who takes a decidedly low-key approach to pushing his clients. Tom Cruise, on the other hand, who was also handled by Pat until the summer of 2004, was written up in the venerable *New York Times* in 2002 for being overexposed. Previously, Cruise had been considered a slam dunk in terms of being a "get"—when he graced the cover of *Vanity Fair* in February 2002, newsstand sales skyrocketed. But he saw his PR clout plummet after serial covers on *W*, *Entertainment Weekly*, *Time*, and others. In fact, *Entertainment Weekly*'s editor was so annoyed at having to share his cover subject with so many others that he predicted Tom would have to go into hiding for a while to get over it. My feeling is that once you are too available, people get sick of you (particularly if you are Tom Cruise, and therefore slightly dull to begin with).

Some say overexposure is to blame for the rapid decline of Ricky Martin, and for all of the speculation about whether Britney's career is over. For three years Britney seemed to have the world by the tail— hell, even Madonna wore a T-shirt with her name on it. And yet her third album ended up selling less than her first two, precisely because you couldn't get away from her.

Another publicity mistake is mismanaging a potentially damaging PR crisis. I have never understood why some publicists respond to such events by not responding (i.e., not returning phone calls, or saying nothing at all). Which, to me, means they are being paid sometimes thousands of dollars a month to neglect a basic function of their job. Usually all this does is give the columnist a chance to print just one side of the story. At least call and give us a good old "no comment."

Another big no-no—we touched on it earlier—is blatant lying. Robert Garlock, a publicist for PMK-HBH, Pat Kingsley's firm, has blatantly lied in the past and therefore his word is taken with a whole heap of salt. He told me Uma Thurman and Ethan Hawke were not separating the summer of 2003 (they were) and that Tom Cruise and Penelope Cruz hadn't split by Oscars 2004 (they had). So I put him in the paper, branding him a liar, and now, when Page Six has a story about one of Robert's clients and Robert denies it, we note, "Robert Garlock, a known liar, denies the story," which puts a cloud of doubt over anything Robert says.

Good publicists know how to avoid this at all costs. For example, when Julia Roberts and Danny Moder had their quickie wedding on July 4, 2002, Julia's PR woman, Marcy Engelman, may have never actually lied when she told the *Daily News* that Julia "was not getting married that weekend. She'll be in the Hamptons." Marcy wasn't lying, because she claims she didn't know about the wedding until the day before it happened. After she found out, she stopped answering calls from the press, which was a good strategy. That way she didn't have to confirm or deny or lie.

At Page Six we have something called the Liar's Corner, which is where, whenever a PR person lies to us, we print their name and offense. Liar's Corner came about thanks to Penelope Cruz's PR man, Robert Garlock. After repeatedly lying to us over the years and costing us several scoops, we'd finally had it. After he once again was caught in a lie, and cost us the Tom Cruise/Penelope Cruz split scoop, we printed this: ". . . Not that Cruz has been unhappy over the breakup. As the McConaughey pal points out, 'One man drinks, smokes and has a ball, and the other is a robot.' Penelope is having the time of her life." It was McConaughey who helped his newfound "friend" Cruz through an injury on the Moroccan set and provided solace when her father fell ill.

Cruise, meanwhile, was busy publicizing his movie *The Last Samurai*. Cruise, who celebrated the announcement of his split with Cruz by dining with Will Smith at Spice Market Thursday night, has yet to be linked to another woman. But the star won't be unattached for long, and Hollywood insiders speculate his next escort will likely be a Scientologist, because Cruise has been devoting more time to his faith and surrounding himself with fellow Scientologists.

Cruz's rep, Robert Garlock, denied the affair. But everything Garlock says should be taken with several grains of salt, as he has often lied about his celebrity clients, who include Cruz, Uma Thurman, Johnny Depp, Hugh Grant, Calista Flockhart and Kate Winslet. When Page Six called about the demise of the Cruz/Cruise relationship in early February, Garlock swore the two were together and happy. In fact, they had already split. Before Cruz and Cruise hooked up, Page Six said Cruz was shacking up with her *Captain Corelli's Mandolin* co-star Nicolas Cage, and later, with *All the Pretty Horses* co-star Matt Damon. Garlock denied both stories, which were true. Last August, Garlock also denied our story that Thurman had split with Ethan Hawke—even though the two were in fact over.

McConaughey's representative, Alan Nierob, an honest publicist with integrity, "declined comment." Believe me when I say that publicists are much more truthful with us since we started Liar's Corner. Thanks Robert!

Trust me: When lied to, the press turns ruthless. Aaron Mathias, an aspiring actor, hired the wrong publicist and found out the hard way. His PR team told gossip columnists all over town that Mathias was dating Mariah Carey, when a) he wasn't and b) they double planted (didn't make the item exclusive to one gossip column). Fortunately for Page Six, it was Rush & Molloy who ended up falling for the lie and printing the story, which just made them look silly. Cindi Berger, Mariah's invariably tough and honest PR person, said the story was hogwash, which it was. I am sure Rush & Molloy were not pleased.

Another example of this has to do with the wedding of Matt LeBlanc, of *Friends*. Obviously, there was a lot of media interest in this event. I got the word late on a Thursday, and called LeBlanc's press guy, Joe, and said: "Hey, I hear Matt is getting married in Hawaii this weekend." Joe answered, "Really, I didn't hear that. I heard it was Jennifer Lopez and Ben Affleck." After snooping around for a bit, I called Joe back and said: "Joe, I am writing that Matt is getting married this weekend and I need a comment from you. I also need to tell you that if you lie to me and say he isn't getting married and he does, you will henceforth be referred to in Page Six until the end of time as 'Joe, a known liar.' Now what is your comment?" To which Joe sighed and mumbled, "No comment," which should be noted is not a lie. Of course it turned out that Matt LeBlanc did indeed get married that weekend in Hawaii.

What if someone calls you about a story you didn't want out there? Still no reason to lie. Need I say "Bill Clinton"? Matthew Rich observes, "It's better to come clean. When you're caught, you're caught. Hollywood has been using this tactic for a long time. 'Okay, I'm a drug addict. I'm an alcoholic. I'm going into rehab. I'm going to be better.' Everybody loves that kind of story, in a way."

The truth will not only set you free, it will steer you away from the rage of a vindictive press. Sometimes, if the situation is truly horrendous, just retreat for a while. That's why St. Barth's exists! Wait for a bigger story to come along, and then sneak back.

How do you break up with your publicist if and when the time comes? Don't burn your bridges. If you feel the need to move on, be professional, direct, and courteous about it. I can give you personal examples of how a pissed-off PR person has sought—and usually gotten—their revenge; however, I won't, because I don't want to piss them off—and our conversations were off the record. Remember, one bad brick can ruin the foundation of your career. And you don't need someone who knows all your secrets blabbing them to everyone.

A word about comebacks and false starts. Let's say you've gotten your fifteen minutes of fame and now you're on the road to nowhere. Or no matter how hard you try, you can't seem to get up and running in the first place. I have a piece of advice for you: DON'T GIVE UP. IT'S NOT OVER 'TIL IT'S OVER, AND NOT EVEN THEN! I have mentioned again and again the importance of tenacity and persistence. Think about George Clooney. He had thirteen TV pilots canceled before hitting pay dirt with *ER*. James Gandolfini worked for more than twenty years as an actor before landing the Tony Soprano role that has given him immortality.

Kim Cattrall of *Sex and the City* is another example of someone who never gave up. She was considered over the hill by Hollywood standards when she scored the role of Samantha. Now she has more scripts offered to her than she can possibly read.

It wasn't too long ago when people thought John Travolta's career was over. He had starred in *Grease* and *Saturday Night Fever*, but was well on his way to being pronounced washed up when he got his role in *Pulp Fiction*, a performance that sent critics swooning and brought audiences back to the altar.

Robert Evans's book *The Kid Stays in the Picture* is precisely about this phenomenon. At the time of its publication, Evans was widely considered not only a "has-been," but a has-been who had been involved in a murder trial. Then in 2000, his memoir caught the eye of *Vanity Fair* editor Graydon Carter, who was looking to branch out into film production and decided his first project would be Evans's autobiography. After the premiere, Robert once again became the toast of Tinseltown.

But perhaps the biggest recent comeback of all was that of Liza Minnelli. In 2000, she was overweight, depressed, confined to a wheelchair. According to several tabloids, she "almost died," not once but several times, and suffered a life-threatening stroke. Even then, she wasn't considered press-worthy. But everything changed after Liza and David Gest met at a Michael Jackson concert. They "fell in love," got married, and once again Liza became a boldfaced name. I wish I could say they lived happily ever after.

And when you are not in a business that "takes off" overnight, it is harder. Say you are a cattle farmer outside of Omaha. That is a business that needs years of development (and cattle breeding), so patience is a must. But remember, there are always things you can do to get your name out there. At the next livestock show, buy a billboard, get an article written about you in *Farmer's Almanac*, or auction off a prized cow as a gimmick.

If you are a teacher in Columbus, Ohio, and want to get elected to the city council, start showing up at meetings and being vocal. Volunteer in your community and become active in your union. You most likely won't be noticed overnight, because a good reputation takes time to build. But when you do make a run for office, you will be noticed and remembered for your hard work and effort.

Don't forget: There's always hope and there's always tomorrow.

## Chapter Six

# How the Press Works, and How You Can Work It

T HIS CHAPTER IS RELATED TO THE LAST ONE, BUT IT delves more deeply into the actual workings of the press. You will see a real benefit to your marketing and PR efforts if you understand how the press works and how, in turn, to work it.

"Press is the water and the air of fame and power," says Couri Hays, who should know. "You can't get elected without it, you can't sell a movie ticket without it—nowadays you can't sell a cookie without it. If you're in a town of forty and you're the local hairdresser, you want good press."

Good press that will spread the word about how brilliant your movie is, what a fabulous book you've written, what luxurious spa services you offer, how wonderful the food is at your new restaurant. While good press can make you, bad press can break you. Bad press can close a Broadway show overnight, end a socialite's tenure on the A-list, and even be the nail in the coffin of a troubled marriage. It's not just the president of the United States and Martha Stewart who can find their world turned upside down by bad press.

While the fourth estate as a group prides itself on its objectivity and independence, there are real, concrete ways of using the press to your advantage, and I'm going to let you in on these tricks of the trade.

### 1. Learn the Timeline.

I work for a daily newspaper, and in New York City, we are not the only game in town. There are several other dailies, as well as a variety of weekly newspapers. We probably have more than our share of papers in the Big Apple, but every town has its own local rags, as well as the handful of nationally distributed newspapers, such as the *Wall Street Journal* and *USA Today*. These papers, along with magazines and the wire services, comprise what is commonly known as "print." (We'll get to TV and other broadcast media later.)

Most print falls into the categories of daily, weekly, or monthly, described as such because of their deadlines and how often they are published. In general, if you are working to get yourself press, your best bet will be the daily newspapers, since they continually need to feed the beast; that is, they have a constant, insatiable need for copy to fill their pages. Alternative weekly papers, such as the *Chicago Reader*, the *Village Voice*, and *L.A. Weekly*, are also often receptive to good pitches about local events, products, or people, and they are more likely to be interested in something new and as yet undiscovered. It is sad but true that many big city papers will only pick up a story that has already been written about somewhere else. At the *Post* we have a joke about the *New York Times*'s coverage outside of Section A: "It's not news unless it's already been out in other media for a month." It's a bandwagon effect. One newspaper sees what another paper is doing and doesn't want to be out-scooped, and therefore covers the same territory or event.

---

The tidal wave effect, or it all starts with a drop in the pond effect: Get your name in print somewhere. Then use that mention to pitch your story to a bigger publication. Use the second mention to get into a larger local daily paper, then head for a local weekly. After a few of these local mentions pile up, you are ready to take aim at regional or national print and television. The biggest tidal wave can be started by the smallest ripple.

---

Let's say you are an emerging artist in Cincinnati, Ohio. You have finally managed to get a gallery to display your work, but you don't want to depend on the young, overworked staff of the gallery (if there is a staff) to make sure the press shows up. Naturally you will want the two big local papers, the *Cincinnati Enquirer* and the *Cincinnati Post*, to review your exhibit or cover your gallery opening, but that may be unrealistic. It would be more likely that the alternative weekly, *City Beat*, would be interested in the exhibit and send a hungry freelancer out to write about it. An article in the *Beat* will start the buzz ball rolling; you can take that piece and use it to get additional coverage. Send the piece out to local radio stations, to magazines that list events, to local TV. Show them it's a real story worth covering.

Obviously it is a lot easier to garner local press coverage than to land a piece in a national periodical. However, nationals often look to local magazines and newspapers for story ideas, and that is another way to use the local coverage you have received. Put together a "press packet" of the press clippings you've garnered and send it with a pitch letter to the reporter most likely to be interested at the national press outlet you've chosen to target. That's how top publicists do it—why not adopt their tried-and-true methods?

A good pitch letter will grab the reader right away. Don't spend a lot of time beginning the letter with introductions or by over-explaining. Get right to the point. There is an old rule of journalism: "Don't bury your lead." Pack the first part of the pitch with reasons why your event or story is something unusual and great, something the reporter should cover. Will there be prominent people in attendance? Are you raising money for a charity? Will there be giveaways of interest? Is it controversial? Groundbreaking? Uplifting? Hook them with the first sentence and then reel them in.

---

Don't Bury the Lead! At the *Post* we have a rule: If you can't tell what a story is trying to say by the end of the first two (and preferably, just the first) paragraphs, it's not worth reading. You have to be immediately sucked in. When preparing the pitch for the story you want to sell, make sure you get your point across quickly and concisely. People have very short attention spans, and reporters' are even shorter.

---

Stu Bykofsky, who writes for the *Philadelphia Daily News*, recalls that when his bosses at the paper told him his beat would be writing about Philadelphia celebrities, he realized he was being told to "write about celebrities in a town that didn't have any." His solution? "I invented them."

---

Big fish: Is it good to be a big fish in a small pond? Yes. Even if your desire is to reach a national audience, you should start by thinking locally. Remember, the tallest skyscrapers arise from solid, sturdy foundations.

---

Stu has carved out a great niche writing about the local television station weathermen, athletes on local teams, members of city council. The point is that there is more of a chance to get a high level of exposure in a medium- or small-sized city or town, if you know how to go about attracting it. Do your homework. Realize that every newspaper has a desire to be "in the know," to have its finger on the community pulse.

So how do you present yourself, or whatever you are promoting, as something newsworthy, a discovery worth making, the coolest thing out there? First, identify precisely what it is you are trying to sell. If you are a local politician running for town council, like Diane Skudlarek of North Wales, Pennsylvania, you are selling your image, your credibility, your work ethic. Diane took a good, hard look in the mirror and realized that while she looked like she would be right at home at the opening of the hottest music club in Philadelphia, her somewhat edgy, hip look was not as well suited to the world of local politics in conservative Bucks County. So she adopted a more traditional hairstyle, began to wear nicely tailored suits and shoes with lower heels, and toned down her makeup. When she went out to meet potential voters, she worked on projecting confidence and experience, choosing not to emphasize her youthful looks. While looking younger than your age is an asset in many places, it is not necessarily a plus when you're trying to be taken seriously in politics. She got friends and family to volunteer to help put up signs, and to host teas and cocktail parties. Once this engine was started, Diane contacted the appropriate political reporters in the local media and told them about the platform she was running on. She talked about the issues and went on the attack about her competitor's record. And she won, despite being a Democrat running in a heavily Republican county. She garnered a huge amount of ink, for a "newbie."

Once you've figured out what you're promoting and what your presentation is going to be, you need to learn about what sort of deadlines the print media work under, and how to make it into their pages.

You should know that beginning at about three or four o'clock every afternoon, most newsrooms at daily papers are in a state of absolute chaos. They are approaching deadline and everyone is scrambling to finish their stories. When someone calls me at, say, 5 P.M. to plug something, my instinctive response is to hang up on them. I don't enjoy being rude or obnoxious, but at this time of day, my editor is invariably yelling at me, and I often have at least two or three items I still need to finish, and my blood pressure is climbing by the second. I would be much more receptive to your pitch if you were to call me between ten in the morning and one in the afternoon. During this time, I am already out of my morning meeting where we discuss the stories we are working on for the day, and I'm still casting about for more things to write about. If you call me at four or five, you better be telling me that Paris Hilton has entered a convent, or that Russell Crowe and Meg Ryan are back together. Otherwise, you just don't understand my job and how to do business with me, and I will probably not be buying what you're selling. This holds true for most of my colleagues too.

---

Daily deadlines: I can't impress this upon you enough. By 5 P.M., daily newspaper writers are in a panic. DO NOT BOTHER THEM! By and large, a newspaper writer will arrive at the office between 10 and 11 A.M. Start the calls or pitches around 1 P.M., after they have had time to settle, have lunch, and are feeling curious. Think of it almost like a lion cub in the zoo. After it has slept, fed, and bathed, it is ready for some action.

---

At weekly publications, on the other hand, deadlines vary. If a newspaper appears on newsstands on Wednesdays, as the *New York Observer* does, don't call that publication on Monday, when the staff is probably in high panic mode, trying to close the week's edition. Instead, call on Thursday, when the writers are just starting to think about what to cover for next week's edition. Find out the paper's "deadline" (you can just call and ask what it is) and go from there. For monthly magazines, deadlines are usually two, three, or even four months ahead of the issue date. This means that if you are trying to get something into one of these publications, you have to work far ahead, and you also have to be creative.

Here's how New York socialite Helen Lee Schifter approached the task of getting press. In the nineties, Helen met and married Tim Schifter, the wealthy owner of LeSportsac. Helen then got jobs at *Mademoiselle* and *Vogue*. But Helen wanted an identity apart from being a magazine drone and "wife of." She wanted to be one of those beautiful women whose photographs frequently grace the pages of glossy fashion and lifestyle magazines (like the ones she worked at), and so she did the following. She already knew many of the photographers whose pictures are regularly used by magazines and newspapers, people like Bill Cunningham of the *New York Times*, or Patrick McMullen. She is known for her impeccable taste in fashion, and she always looks great in whatever she is wearing. Whenever she went out, she made a point of finding the photographer and sort of dancing and twirling and posing in front of him, giving him a great photo op. This got her into the *Times*, *Women's Wear Daily*, and the like.

But to permanently establish herself as a fashionista she went a step further. Every year, there are two major fashion seasons, and therefore two major New York fashion show seasons, spring and fall. Held in specially erected tents in midtown Manhattan's Bryant Park, the spring fashion shows take place in September, the fall shows in February. These are huge extravaganzas, and everyone who is anyone gets dressed to the nines and hopes to merit a front-row seat. In her campaign for coverage, Helen used her knowledge of magazines' early deadlines to her advantage. She would arrive at the February show amid the snow drifts and icy winds wearing a slip of a spring dress, knowing that when the magazines would be running their coverage of the spring fashions a few months later, they would be looking for people wearing something that looked like it belonged in the spring season. She would go to five or six shows in one day, always changing outfits in between shows so as not to be photographed twice in the same outfit—and to increase her chances of being published.

---

Helen's Butterfly Effect: Like a butterfly emerging from its cocoon, Helen knew everyone would be delighted by her pretty wings. So emerge from your cocoon like a beautiful butterfly every time you walk out of your front door. You will be rewarded for making the extra effort.

---

Guess what? It worked. Today Helen is a regular on best-dressed lists. She went from being a relatively obscure fashion watcher to a front-row fixture in the space of just a few years simply by using her knowledge of the press.

Anyone can learn important lessons from what she did. If you are a florist, find out when your local paper is putting together a special wedding supplement and then pitch them a story about your fabulous bridal bouquets before their deadline. If you own a costume shop, prepare a photo op that can be used at Halloween. Think ahead. Plan ahead. Devise a strategy. Do your homework!

## 2. *Pitch to the Right Player.*

Carefully read papers and magazines to learn who covers what, in order to decide which reporter might be most receptive to your pitch.

Use basic common sense. A gossip writer is not a fashion reporter. A features editor probably doesn't have anything to do with listings. One of the most annoying things to any press person is getting a call from someone who has obviously never read a word of his or her work, section, or at times, entire newspaper. Yet they want to be included in it.

This is pretty basic but important stuff. If you are a woodworker launching a new furniture line, you shouldn't be calling the news desk with your information unless you have just been robbed by three large men with guns who turned out to be part of the Jesse James gang.

However, you may find success with the house and home section of the paper, or perhaps the features section, if you are creative enough to come up with a story line for them. For example, say you are a female contractor who teaches classes to women on how to do their own plumbing. Your pitch might be: Female homebuilder teaches local women to plumb for themselves. Be ready to back up your pitch with a press kit, including a bio, a business description, photos of you and your work, and any other press clips, if you have them.

Chris Gardner works for the West Coast office of *People* magazine. He points out that journalists have egos, and that if you want to make headway with them, it is best to approach them already clearly knowing what their beat is and what they've recently written. He told me: "I get this all the time. People ask me to do things and I'm like, 'Do you even know where I work? We would never write something like that!'" On the other hand, he continues, "If you're like: 'Hey, I noticed you did this column and I have this cool story for you. I don't know if you'd be interested in it, but it fits with what you've covered before and it might work,' that sort of knowledge gets you in so much quicker." In other words, if you call a journalist without knowing what they write about, you are basically telling them: "Hey, you don't know me and I've never read your work, but I'd like you to do me a favor." (The answer to that is almost always no.)

Chris Gardner, like many of us in this business, is actually a softie at heart, and he likes it when people show some initiative and are knowledgeable about what they're saying. "I kind of love it when people call. I wrote this little thing called the Rep

Sheet, which is made up of agency/client signings. When people call me themselves and say, 'Hey, I just signed with an agent. Can you put it in your column?' I always do it for them. They actually took the initiative to look me up and call for themselves, and not have somebody else do it for them."

So before you make that important call, READ THE NEWSPAPER OR MAGAZINE YOU WANT TO GET INTO FIRST! Figure out exactly where you or your story would fit in, and then GO FOR IT!

### 3. Perfect Your Pitch.

There are some basic rules of thumb for pitching Page Six, where I work, that also hold true for pretty much every other column across the country. We've already addressed the fact that lying is a mortal sin. But double planting comes close in terms of what we don't want. For the uninitiated, double planting is when someone offers me an item and simultaneously offers it to another columnist at a different publication. If I decide to write it up and the other columnist does too, we both look stupid. Journalists want and expect exclusives!

I have learned this business from some of the best, including my boss, Richard, and from the two *grande dames* of gossip, the *Post*'s Cindy Adams and Liz Smith. They are my colleagues, but they are also the competition. The *Post*'s main outside competition is the *New York Daily News*, which has two gossip columns. Their main column is written by the husband-and-wife team of Rush & Molloy, and their second column is currently being written by former *Washington Post* writer Lloyd Grove (this second column at the *Daily News* tends to change hands frequently). Even the *New York Times* has a daily gossip column, "Boldface Names," and the much smaller *Newsday* runs Liz Smith's syndicated column as well as a weekly dish section. With all of us out there, the competition in New York to get the best gossip first is fierce.

For more than fifteen years under my boss Richard Johnson's eye, Page Six has established itself as the most competitive and newsworthy of all these gossip columns, breaking nearly all the major gossip stories that are later carried in national newspapers and magazines. The key to our edge is exclusivity. Believe me when I say that nothing irks us more than publishing a bit of gossip we think is exclusive and then having it show up in Rush & Molloy too.

The 10 Commandments of Pitching a Story

1. Thou shall not lie.
2. Thou shall not steal . . . anyone else's ideas.
3. Thou shall not double plant with a competing paper or columnist.
4. Thou shall pitch interesting and newsworthy stories!
5. Thou shall not call at deadline unless it is Armageddon.
6. Thou shall not covet anyone else's press, because you can always go out and get even better for yourself!
7. Thou shall learn that e-mail is a blessed thing. Those damned phones never shut up! Do us all a favor and send an e-mail.
8. Thou shall learn how to spot interesting stories by reading articles the paper currently publishes.
9. Thou shall not ramble and otherwise waste our time.
10. Thou shall not say stupid things like, "Don't believe what you read in the press." Always believe the press! Hell, we're the ones held

to libel and legal standards, not the crazy
conspiracy-theory lady you always talk to
who lives down the street!

---

If we do find that someone has double planted,
they are banned (at least temporarily, depending on
how good the source is) from the page. Period. It is
also a no-no, even though we are all in the same
family, to give something to Page Six and simultaneously to Cindy or Liz, or to any other section of
the *Post*, for that matter. It is a waste of everyone's
time. Working on something another section of the
paper is also working on is frustrating, mainly because we could have been digging up another story
instead. Pick one person and stick with them, unless
they have definitively passed on your item.

My boss, Richard, says: "I hate publicists who lie.
And I am always amazed at the sort of duplicity that
goes on. You think you have a scoop and then it
turns out the *Daily News* has the same story on the
same day. Now, I wonder how they got that—just
dumb luck? No, it's because some scheming publicist figures 'I can make points with Rush & Molloy
because I know Page Six has a story coming out. I
know this because they called me asking about it. So

I'll call Rush & Molloy and say 'I know that Page Six has a story coming out. I'll let you have it, and you're gonna owe me big time.'"

Richard is still smarting over the Liza Minnelli and David Gest divorce story. He had gotten the scoop that the odd couple of the century were splitting and then saw it miraculously appear in Rush & Molloy the next day. He has a good idea of who whispered our exclusive story to the competition, and that person is now blackballed.

So now you know not to commit these cardinal sins, but what are we actually looking for? Keep in mind that almost everyone enjoys a good character. You or your client may not be famous, but if there is something really interesting, unique—even bizarre—about you, play it up! Anna Wintour, the editor of *Vogue*, has gotten tons of press just because she rarely takes off her sunglasses. Steven Cojocaru (now at *Entertainment Tonight*) is nothing if not a character and we love him for it. Don't be boring!

Case in point: Paris Hilton. Some people may have wondered just where the hell Miss Hilton came from when the national media started bombarding them with photos of the scantily clad blonde in early 2003. And then, with stories about her amateur porn video.

And most recently, with her stunningly stupid TV show, *The Simple Life*.

In fact, my boss Richard has been writing about Paris in Page Six since she was only sixteen and making her society debut dancing on tabletops in clubs wearing no panties (and getting caught on camera). He laughs, "Without Page Six constantly reporting on her doings, nobody would have been interested in Paris going down to a farm. I think that maybe she wants more attention than the other pretty socialites, and she loves posing for pictures. It was hard to miss her." He offers: "There are certain people who are funny and fun, and smart, and who you figure deserve press. And there are others who are boring, social climbing, and vulgar, who don't."

Do you perhaps have a trademark look or quality, a signature style or gesture, something that sets you apart from the rest that you could use to position yourself in the press? This might be easier to achieve in some places than in others, as Sasha Issenberg points out. Sasha himself is something of a journalism prodigy. He started out in college writing for *George*, the now defunct political magazine started by John Kennedy, Jr. After *George* folded, Sasha moved to Philadelphia to become a staff writer at *Philadelphia* magazine. He confirms that it is a lot easier to get press attention in a city that is the size of Philadelphia than it is in New York. As proof, Sasha cites John Bolaris, now WCBS-TV New York's weatherman, as someone who used being a bit of a character around Philly to his advantage. Back when Bolaris was working for a Philadelphia television station, he became one of the city's most recognized personalities. "He was a single guy who was not afraid to be seen out in public with a wide array of women. He became famous for over-hyping this would-be storm of the century a few years ago that ended up being nothing. For a week the station was promoting this storm that was going to be so devastating, and it never materialized. There was this ongoing thing where John was wearing a black turtleneck on the air all the time. His director told him not to wear it anymore. The turtleneck became his look. He stood up for the turtleneck. On his last day on the air, the sports anchor also wore a turtleneck, "in solidarity."

Here you have a guy who became a local celebrity primarily by cultivating his own look, not being shy about expressing his personality, even if it was goofy, and therefore stood out a little from the crowd. That in turn made a bigger station in a bigger market want his kind of star power working for them. The moral of this story is: figure out what you can cultivate in yourself that will make you stand out, and WORK IT!

**4. All we want is a good, satisfying story, like the kind your mother used to tell you at night.**

It really helps a writer if the story you are pitching comes ready-made (and stands up under confirmation).

When it comes to a gossip item, here's some advice from the best: Richard Johnson. He says, "An item is the sort of thing you would tell at a dinner table to your friends. A funny story, one that will get a laugh. Something that everybody at the table is interested in. It's not like 'so-and-so celebrity had dinner at a restaurant.' There's no punch line to that. The story doesn't go anywhere. I keep trying to explain to publicists that what we really want are stories. Stories have a beginning and they have an end. Some sort of drama is involved. Even suspense, maybe."

---

Press whores: We all know them. Those annoying people who will do *anything* to get in the paper! There is a fine line between getting press and whoring yourself out to get it. Don't cross that line!

---

Michael Klein, who works at the *Philadelphia Inquirer*, offers this advice: "Be lively. Tell people things they don't know . . . tell little stories." Local people catch Klein's eye by "doing something different."

Of course, just as no two readers are the same, no two reporters will totally agree on what most bugs them, or what most makes their day. What are some individual pet peeves? *Premiere* magazine's Howard Karren says, "The biggest problem people have is not being able to perceive themselves the way others perceive them. So you'll get people calling in and wanting to either write or be published or be recognized in some way and they have absolutely no sense of how uninteresting that is to 99.99 percent of anybody who would pick up a magazine." He says getting it right is partly instinctual: "You have to be able to take yourself out of yourself and look at a newspaper or magazine and think, 'What would I want to read?' If you didn't know yourself and you heard this story, would you still be interested in it?"

My pal Chris Gardner, who used to work at the *Hollywood Reporter* writing mostly about film, film stars, and people who want to get into film, now works in the west coast bureau of *People*. He told me that the people who get his attention, besides the obviously famous, are those "who have really worked hard to get where they are, and they may only have one or two credits, but maybe those one or two credits really sparked you. Like wow—they have really great taste, they have chosen really good roles . . . I want to know more about that person and I want to write about them."

I'm convinced that everybody has a good story. (Or almost everyone—some people never move from their couch in front of the TV set except to go to the bathroom or the refrigerator—those people have to get a life!)

I have a friend named Amy Sacco. She is a 6-foot-2-inch blonde bombshell (they really do exist) who owns two of the hottest clubs in Manhattan, Lot 61 and Bungalow 8. She is widely viewed as the nightlife queen of New York City. One night at Lot 61, over many cocktails, Amy told me how she approaches being interviewed. She tells reporters, "I'm a truck driver's daughter from New Jersey who made it on my own in New York. And that's all true. I just don't tell them my dad owned the business!"

Amy is smart. She knows everyone loves a rags-to-riches tale, a good, old-fashioned Little Orphan Annie story. Let's face it. No one really loves the person whose father gave them everything. So with just a little twist, Amy turns her story into one that is a feel-good version of the American Dream.

### 5. *Create your own storyline.*

Be smart, be creative, and keep in mind who you want to bite.

Couri Hay suggests that a client start off by doing "something important, something worthwhile. Do something that gives something to others. I think that's what gets you noticed. Be a Good Samaritan. Do a good deed—that's a great way to get good press. Then, of course, look good—and take your top off!" Joke.

But seriously, folks, Couri goes on, "Just be the best you can be and eventually, if you've learned to be in the right place at the right time in the right outfit with the right people, someone is gonna notice. If you look good enough they'll take your picture. Learn to give a good quote." It also helps to have a specific area of expertise. Become the go-to person about makeup, or politics, or food, or what everyone's reading that season. Be prepared to say in a sentence or two who you are and what you do, and to make it sound interesting. And if that doesn't work, there's always the old standby: quid pro quo.

### 6. *Quid pro quo.*

We have room for several different levels and types of stories in Page Six. There is one big lead item, a larger double, and several small items. A few times a week we run something called "sightings," as in "Robert Downey, Jr., spotted at Lacoste putting $100,000 on his American Express" or "Nan Kempner eating piles of food at the Times Square Olive Garden." Then there are the "we hear" items, as in "We hear that the National Garden Society is having its fundraiser tonight at the Winter Garden" or "We hear that our favorite off-Broadway play is going weekly, every Friday night."

Why do we run these items? They are favors. You scratch my back and I'll scratch yours. For example, someone calls up and says they saw Katie Couric having lunch with CBS head Les Moonves. This comes just after word's leaked out that Katie Couric's contract with NBC is almost up. The person who called in with the item follows that with a casual: "Hey, is there any way you could possibly fit in a mention of my new baked goods that will be sold in Wal-Mart starting in May?" I might be able to work in the lousy baked goods mention because you gave me the Katie Couric item.

But sometimes quid pro quo can become quid

pro *bad*. For example, consider my experience with a young publicist who used to work at a large PR firm. Let's call her Betty. Betty and I both started our respective jobs at around the same time. At first she worked on bottom-rung showbiz clients, or corporate accounts like Motorola. Because I felt sorry for her I used to print her sightings and "we hears" as a favor, without getting or expecting anything in return. But one day she finally did start representing big stars like Nicole Kidman and Vin Diesel. Did she return the favors? No. Instead, she was always uncooperative, stopped returning Page Six's calls, and even tried keeping me out of certain parties (which she was unable to do, by the way). Now, when I have to speak with her regarding one of her clients, I do it, but as far as any favor is concerned, forget it. Life is long, and so is my memory.

### 7. Use the paparazzi.

When most people hear the word "paparazzi" they think of rabid hordes of photographers staking out a celebrity's home, or the throngs of clickers outside a restaurant where celebs are trying, and failing, to have a private moment. That is definitely an element of the paparazzi, but here I'm talking about those photographers who can help you get your image into the paper.

It's no accident that certain actresses, models, and socialites are regularly photographed, and it's not always just because they're the most beautiful or the biggest stars. Our friend in L.A. Chris Gardner mentioned Brittany Murphy as a good example of someone who has employed the paparazzi to her advantage. "She totally works the paparazzi . . . laughing and hugging people and even jumping into their arms. Those are the kinds of crazy photos people want to put on the society pages of their magazines because they're cool, because they're different, because they're wacky."

Couri Hay cites good old Paris Hilton as "the perfect example of somebody who has learned how to capture the attention of the world through photos. Sex still sells. And so does chic. There are women in New York like Muffy Potter Aston or Brooke Astor who are chic. They have impeccable taste . . . impeccable manners. That's another way to get noticed. Be polite . . . So you can either take all your clothes off, or you can dress really well."

Besides stripping down or otherwise acting in a manner that would cause your mother to hide her face in shame, there are other ways to attract the paparazzi. Learn to anticipate what sort of picture a photographer will be looking for at an event. Spring 2004 saw an event in New York called Dressed to Kilt, a Scottish fashion show extravaganza and charity event. There were many people in the room wearing regular plaid kilts and otherwise looking generically Scottish, but two women had clearly gone to a lot of trouble to get noticed. They wore stunning, flowing gowns made out of gorgeous tartan plaids, and they stood posing side by side whenever possible, especially when there was a camera nearby.

They stood out, and they were giving the photographers the picture they had come out to the event to capture. Every paper and magazine has a photographer in their employ whose job it is to take snaps at events like this. Find out who it is and learn to recognize them. They offer you a great publicity opportunity.

## 8. *What if it all goes horribly wrong?*

So you've done your homework, perfected your pitch, had your picture taken, and gotten a writer to agree to cover your art opening. Your new chocolate baskets are going to be featured in all the holiday gift sections right before Christmas. Somehow, though, the writer gets your name wrong, gives your competitor's phone number, and mistakenly implies that your chocolates contain laxatives and arsenic. What do you do now?

If, unlike this example, the mistake is relatively minor and not serious, try to shrug it off. For all of the work it takes to get something written about, the other side of the coin is that today's newspaper is tomorrow's birdcage liner. If you feel it's important to inform the writer that a mistake was made, try to do it in a polite and professional way. Do not start screaming. Keep a cool head. Ask that the paper run a correction, but remember: Keeping your cool always works better than losing it, and you always get more flies with honey.

If you have tried to reason with the writer, but for whatever reason he is being unresponsive and you genuinely feel a correction is imperative, go to his editor. Clearly explain what was factually wrong with the story. Then ask for a published correction. If there has been a catastrophic mistake that has affected your business, contact a lawyer. Do this only as a last resort.

Now, go out there with confidence and get yourself in print!

Summer doldrums, winter blues: Summer is slow and winter has no light. So liven up the day and brighten up the darkness with your stories!

## Chapter Seven

# The Power of TV

Listen. I am from Ohio. So I know—I mean, I KNOW—how important television is. When I was growing up, our celebrities were the local newscasters and local girls in local advertisements. There was even a car dealer with the unfortunate name of Tom Raper who was popular because he put himself in these annoying commercials that aired constantly, especially after the rodeo and monster truck rally broadcasts.

The commercials went something like this: "Come on down to TOM RAPER'S and git your RVs and caravans at low, low prices!" while big neon signs that read "Raper! Raper! Raper!" flashed in the background. It didn't seem to matter that this guy was only famous because he was in his own TV commercial; Tom never waited in line at the local Applebee's, or anywhere else within viewing range of his TV spots.

One winter break during college, I was back in a local bar in Cincinnati when an excited whisper traveled through the crowd: "Oh my God! There's the girl from the JCPenney commercials! She's here! At the bar!" That woman was a star for the night, and was treated like a queen (which in Cincinnati means she got free drinks).

But it's not like that just in Cincinnati. Now more than ever, thanks to reality shows and the proliferation of cable and satellite channels, anyone can achieve fame in what seems like a matter of nanoseconds. Famed PR man Dan Klores, who has been around the block more than a few times and has personally orchestrated numerous journeys into fame, told me about a run-in he recently had with *Bachelorette* star Trista Rehn. Dan went to see the Broadway show *Hairspray* and it turned out that Trista happened to be sitting behind him. Still sounding shocked, Dan says, "Before the show started, the entire theater was taking pictures of her, and were on their cell phones talking about her. She was just on TV trying to find a man—what kind of talent is that? This has all come about because of television."

Dan, who is the publicist for *Saturday Night Live*

among many others, says that when SNL has a guest host who stars on a popular TV show, its ratings are typically higher than when the host is a movie star. In his opinion, today it is television that has the power to create real celebrities.

Chris Gardner of *People* is originally from Iowa. He laughed when I told him what Dan had said, and remarked that one of the most famous people in Des Moines is the guy who picks the lottery numbers live on TV every week.

I may not possess the white-hot fame of the Des Moines Lotto guy, but when I started working for Page Six, I immediately began to get calls inviting me to be a guest on shows like *Entertainment Tonight*, *Inside Edition*, *Access Hollywood*, and *Extra*. In the beginning I loved doing these appearances, even though I wasn't very good at them. But when I realized I was actually working for these shows—and they weren't paying me a cent—I stopped.

The next time an *Extra* producer called me, I said flat out, "I want to get paid." He responded right back, "TV is free publicity. We don't pay anyone who comes on our show because we're doing them a favor." I didn't agree. Up to that point, all I had accrued from appearing on these shows was the reappearance of a bunch of wackos from my past, and once, a phone call from a disturbed New Jersey construction worker who wanted to have sex with me (an offer I declined).

But eventually I met Bradly Bessey, the second in command at *Entertainment Tonight*, who convinced me to work for him for free until he could wrangle me a contract. I—and the *New York Post*—have reaped the benefits of that decision ever since. People all over the country know me now. People in my hometown read my *Post* column online. I have folks calling in gossip from all over the country because they can put a face to my name and feel more comfortable calling me than they would another reporter they've never laid eyes on.

It's funny, because appearing on TV gives a sort of legitimacy to you or your product, even if you are the one paying for the TV spot, as was the case with the aforementioned Mr. Raper. Would anyone out there even know what the hell a Ginsu knife was—not to mention thinking it's the best brand in the business—had the Ginsu people not paid for TV infomercials a long time ago?

The same idea pretty much holds true for Martha Stewart, who ultimately gained credibility, fame, and fortune (and, in the end, some jail time) by going on television with her own show, which was basically an infomercial for herself. TV can launch you or your product in a way nothing else can. Think about the career of Jules Asner. She was a small-time actress when she managed to land a coveted anchor spot on E! network's then little-known show *Wild On*. Two years later, she was anchoring the E! news as well as her own show *Revealed with Jules Asner*. Hello! Who is Jules Asner?? She eventually quit all that to move to New York with her hubby, film director Steven Soderberg, but even after she stopped appearing on TV, she continued to be mobbed by fans and photographers wherever she went, because she had become a permanently boldfaced name. Jules is now back on TV as one of the hosts of *Life & Style*, a knockoff of *The View*.

Much the same thing happened with Ben Curtis, the completely annoying blond dork who became nationally known as the dopey Dell Computer guy. And there are all those previously obscure women on *The View* who gained instant celebrity after Barbara Walters picked them to co-host her daily schmoozefest. I'm not saying it's easy to become your own local version of Dr. Phil. But then again, if you are properly prepared and don't embarrass easily and it's what you really want, it's not impossible either.

Take former federal prosecutor Lis Wiehl. Three

years ago she was merely another lawyer. Then she started appearing on Fox News as a "liberal" counterpoint voice to some of Fox's more conservative hosts. She was smart, well-groomed, and could hold her own against all those shouting men. Today she has a long-term, highly lucrative contract with Fox, and she recently signed a seven-figure, two-book deal with a New York publisher—all the result of that first, successful TV appearance.

And who would ever have heard of Mark Geragos if he hadn't first represented Winona Ryder and therefore posed countless times for the paparazzi? The world's most camera-loving lawyer, though, has to be Gloria Allred, who so loves high-profile cases and the photo ops that come with them that there was even a *South Park* episode devoted to her. The point is, it is essential to use the power of television in a constructive, forward-looking way, a way that helps you get what you want (i.e., not going on *Jerry Springer* and telling your boyfriend you are sleeping with his sister). But first you have to know what the producers are looking for.

### 1. What a Producer Wants

Even for people who are not and have no interest in becoming full-time TV personalities, the boob tube is a phenomenal promotional tool. Nobody knows this better than Bill Shine, Fox News's executive producer—a man who has built his reputation, and Fox News's, on being a "regular" guy. Under the leadership of the infamous Roger Ailes, in five short years Shine and his team overtook longtime leader CNN in ratings, and Fox News now regularly draws double the audience of the much older cable station. The thing to understand about Bill is that he really *is* a regular guy. He didn't graduate from an Ivy League school; he went to the State University of New York at Oswego. And he knows what regular people want. He understands what makes some TV guests shine and others fizzle. But first he has to find them.

Bill explains, "The way we look for guests is like what happens when you drop a rock into a pond, and concentric circles are made. You start in the middle, with the people closest to the story, the principal players. Take the Laci Peterson case. You want to go to family members, to the defense attorneys, to the prosecutors. If for some reason that is not successful, then you go to the next layer, which is personal friends, neighbors. The next layer might be schoolteachers, people who knew her slightly, who used to work with her. I think there were salon people who did her hair. Then you keep going out. Then the outermost circle of all is the pundits. So you just build out, staying as close to the story as possible."

How does this apply to you? It's that outer circle of pundits or experts that you can draw lessons from and become part of. Those people all·had to start somewhere, so where did Shine find them? "The first way in," he told me, "is the concentric circle way. At one point or another, those people were in the first circle off the rock. Gloria Allred, years ago, had a connection to Clinton and Monica and all that stuff. Mark Geragos had his own high-profile cases. In other words, you originally find them because at one point they're in the first circle and now they're in your Rolodex. And since they're in that first circle, then people a) started to know them because they're on a big story, and b) started to know them because they're on TV all the time, and then c) they became savvy. They understood what producers wanted, plus they formed relationships with other producers." Take advantage of the fact that it's a small world!

Once you're in the Rolodex, you stay in the Rolodex . . . at least for a while. I almost never clean out my Rolodex, simply because I don't have any time. The last time I did a purge was because I had to switch to a larger, MONSTER-size Rolodex, and I found cards in there that were practically moth-eaten—many of the contacts had switched jobs five times already since I'd looked at their cards. But the point is, to make it into the Rolodex in the first place, you have to have something to offer in one particular story. Then, to become a contact who gets counted on time and again—someone I can no longer live without—you have to be consistent and show you know what you're doing time and again. Bill Shine and I agree that producers want guests who are smart, who are going to show up prepared, who are not going to arrive two seconds before a live broadcast with stubble and a ripped T-shirt (unless we're talking about Sean Penn). Producers want someone who understands that television is a visual medium, who understands what they are there to say and to say it well, who gives good television. What I mean by that is that if they're going to be on *Hannity & Colmes*, the producer might say: "Hey, just to let you know, this is a debate show. It isn't a show where we just sit around and chat. So please, feel free to jump in if you think the other guest is wrong or spinning you or giving you bullshit." If you're a guest on Bill O'Reilly's show you're going to be told, "Look. Bill is aggressive. If you want to be aggressive in return, go for it, but first make sure you understand Bill O'Reilly. Save your polite, thoughtful persona for Greta Van Susteren."

Howard Karren of *Premiere* concurs. He told me, "What producers are always looking for is someone who's going to connect with the audience in a particular way, whether that means the audience will love them, want to protect them, will be turned on by them, will be fearful of them. This is pretending, of course, that there are a lot of different qualitites in people, even though a tough guy in real life might not be someone who comes off as a tough guy on the screen—these are very different things." He told me that what they're looking for are people "who can translate that quality in a way that makes a performance. What works on camera is something very different from what works in real life."

Carlota Espinosa, a fashion producer for Fox 11 in Los Angeles, is constantly looking for experts who aren't TV personalities to put on the air. What does she want in a guest? "We like people to have fun," she says, "to have a lot of personality. And sure, you have to look camera ready." What does camera ready mean to her? She explains that it's not necessarily how physically attractive the person is. Rather, it's important that they "have a good sense of style."

So what constitutes that TV look?

## 2. Bright Lights, Big Hair

Looking good on TV is different from looking good in real life.

---

TV Trannie Part 2: I'm serious about this. My office at the *New York Post* is in the Fox News building and almost every day I run into anchors like John Gibson, Shepard Smith or Bill O'Reilly. All three of them are pretty masculine manly men, but man, after they have come out of the studio to get a minute of fresh air, they are unrecognizable from all the makeup and hair products! And the ladies are worse. Think of the worst parody of "Harper Valley PTA" and this is what they look like in person with all the TV makeup on. BUT on air, they look normal, almost underdone . . . the lesson here is pile the makeup on for TV, but remember to take it off afterwards.

---

Have you ever seen people just after they've emerged from a TV studio? They often look like drag queens. They are wearing a ton of makeup, which they have to, because one zit looks like leprosy on the small screen. You know those delicate, dark circles under your eyes, the ones some guy told you were smoky and seductive? On television they make you look like a hollow-eyed skeleton. Everything about you is exaggerated, amplified, and exacerbated. The adage that TV adds ten pounds isn't just an old wives' tale. But I'd say it's more like fifteen.

What about clothes? Bill Shine says he wants people to look like they have "respect" for the show and the audience. But he adds that it all depends on the story. I say picking the right outfit comes down to common sense—and a lot more makeup. Think of it as dressing for a job interview, or picture what your local news anchor might wear on the air and mimic that. And shave! Wash! Smooth down your hair! And don't show too much cleavage unless you're going on Howard Stern!

---

A good sound bite is short, sweet, and to the point. There's an old saying with shows like *Entertainment Tonight*: If they air you talking for more than thirty seconds you did a "Big Segment." My mother always complains that she misses me when I am on the show, but that is because she probably blinked. While I may have taped a segment for thirty minutes to an hour, after editing, I am on the show roughly the same amount of time it takes you to sneeze—although if you do sneeze, you'll miss me! In this day and age, TV programs have about fifty new stories they are trying to pack into a half-hour segment, and the less you say and the more pithy your quote is, the better chance you have to actually make it on air and get called back.

---

### 3. The Art of the Sound Bite

An old trick of giving a good interview is to try and incorporate the question into your answer. Let's say the host begins your segment by saying, "So I hear the hottest thing this year are your hairbands, the ones you've handmade." Your response would be something to the effect of "Well, Jacques, you're right. The hottest thing this year *is* my line of hairbands. They are selling like hotcakes. I can't weave them fast enough! And I do make every single one myself!" The answer to every question must be clear and able to stand alone, because the question itself could be cut from the tape by the time the segment airs. And always use specifics. If someone asks you, for example, about Janet Jackson's breast, don't respond by talking about "her breast." Instead, repeat her name: Always refer to "Janet Jackson's breast." In other words, sound like you know what you're talking about, answer quickly and concisely—no awkward silences—that's called dead air, and it's taboo. Bill Shine refers to that sort of pause as the NASA effect: "Have you ever seen the space shuttle astronauts interviewed live from space?" he asks me. "The anchor goes, 'So you're on this mission to see if ants will reproduce in space.' The director cuts to the astronauts and they're like this: (pause) 'That's right.' Don't do that. When the host asks you a question, don't delay. Answer the question." Mere seconds of "dead air" will cause viewers to change channels.

Michael Musto, the gossip reporter for the *Village Voice*, once wrote an hysterical column on this subject. It started off: "Hello, my name is Michael and I am a soundbite whore. I'm one of those talking heads you see on cable TV giving college-educated opinions about Winona Ryder's meltdown . . . You have to act as if each taping is your star opportunity and sparkle like Kelly Ripa on crack."

Michael was exaggerating slightly for his column, but by and large, he's right. What's more, he is always called back. (You must have seen him and his trademark Coke-bottle glasses on VH-1 or the E! Channel by now!) Talk about a character!

## 4. *The Boy Scout Motto: Be Prepared*

The checklist of TV preparedness

Hair? check
Makeup? check
Suit or other professional attire? check
Something to say? Oops . . .

Remember to research, define, and repeat when on air. Know what you are talking about, say it simply and quickly, and repeat the topic of the question asked.

Always arrive for a television appearance armed with something entertaining and funny to say. Plan it out ahead of time. Howard Karren says, "When you do that, everyone is gratified. Otherwise, it's awkward, there are lulls and spaces and nothing going on. Jim Carrey strikes me as someone who is always prepared.

"When you deal with the press and the public, it's work, it's a job," he cautions. "You are a celebrity, you're a famous person, you are there to dance. Do something. Have something ready. If you don't, people will feel robbed. They'll feel as if they're not getting their money's worth."

And here's something I've learned from personal experience: Keep your hands down. Then you'll let your words shine on their own, instead of coming off like some sort of massively gesticulating performance artist. Above all, know the story! Consider it from all angles, brief the producers or on-air people and see what they're thinking in return. Be able to talk about the subject in large, broad strokes as well as with lots of detail thrown in.

When waiting for the interview to begin, first and most important, RELAX. I don't care how you do it. Cindy Adams, who vies with Liz Smith to be the *grandest dame* on New York gossip, reads poetry out loud to settle her nerves before going on air. In 2002, when the *Post* insisted all columnists get new headshots taken, Cindy waltzed right into the photo studio with her fabulous dog Jazzy (who, sadly, is no longer with us) under one arm and a fur stole on the other. But before the photographer could take the shot, Cindy insisted on taking a few minutes alone to recite poetry to herself, so she could get in the mood. Guess what? She's got the best-looking head-shot at the paper. Her method may seem silly to some, but she got the desired result, and that's what counts.

I remember once going to a VH-1 shoot—I think the segment was on a topic of huge national importance, maybe "Britney: Trash or Treasure?" Usually on a shoot like this, there is a makeup person on set, so before I left home I washed my face, and there wasn't a trace of makeup covering my zits or the bags under my eyes. Five minutes after I walked in, the segment producer came over, looked at me in fright, and asked nervously, ". . . do you have any powder or anything?" To my horror, I realized there was no makeup person, which meant there was also no makeup. I had to go on looking like that. When the segment aired, I was humiliated. I have never looked worse in my life. Even my mother was appalled. I'll never go near a studio again without bringing along an emergency makeup kit (just in case).

## 5. *Getting on the Air*

Just as in the print media, television producers are always looking for a good story. It makes their lives easier if you can provide that story and tell it in an engaging way. And, of course, it's all about making their lives easier.

So where do you find the story if your business is just not that overtly glamorous or unusual? Remember, everyone has a story. The trick is in figuring out how to make it compelling and newsworthy. What if, say, you are a housepainter? Your business is booming, and at the same time, you've been seeing an increase in the amount of graffiti around town. Bill Shine's advice to that housepainter is as follows: "The first thing I would do is get in my car and take pictures of all the graffiti I could find and then e-mail the pictures to the news director—basically, show how graffiti is a problem. Now the local news station has video, and they don't have to send the news crew out to shoot every house. You just saved that guy money—you gave him video." He continues: "I would include a bio of myself, what I can do, why this is a story, and why people would be interested." Now, not only is there a local news angle, but conveniently, you are the expert who can present the solution to the problem. You have to try and be objective about your story, and whether it is newsworthy. This doesn't mean you will get on the air every time, but if you start out thinking of how to make what you're selling into a good story, and by trying to make the producer's job easier, they will be far more willing to hear you out.

How do you bite the bullet and make that first introductory call? Shine admits that on the national level it's very tough if you're not already well known, but he says, "On a local level, you have to remember you're a member of the community—use your connections, or even just drop off a videotape of yourself with a note that says 'Hey, if you ever need anybody . . .'" Of course you could just take a stab in the dark and make a polite introductory phone call, or send an e-mail or letter, but your chances of getting in the door that way are slight. Carlota told me that when she's looking for a new guest she always puts in calls to people she knows to find out who they know. Publicist Couri Hay, who is a frequent television guest and has booked his own clients on countless shows, offers this: "One of the surest ways to get noticed is to know more about something than anyone else. Being an expert is always a sure way to get ahead."

### 6. Good Timing

Just as there is in print media, there is a slow season in television during which producers might be a bit more willing to hear you out—because there's just not much else going on! June, July, and August are the slowest months for television. In the New York area, a lot of the usual suspects are hiding out in the Hamptons and don't want to be bothered, but there are still a lot of hours on TV to fill. So if you can think of the right story, summer might be the ideal time to try and pitch it.

### 7. Are We Live?

Always ask whether an appearance is going to be live or taped before you go on the air. This may seem obvious, but it's worth pointing out. If the interview is taped, at least you know you will have the chance to correct any mistakes. Moreover, out of all of the profound, incisive, and entertaining comments you no doubt said in the course of the taping, the producer will pick the one that makes you look best. But if the action is live, the onus is totally on you. It takes practice to feel confident about appearing on live TV!

### 8. Gotta Have Friends

Once you've finally managed to snag an appearance on your local news or talk show, the next step is . . . to get on again!

Of course you must remember the basics, such as being on time, being prepared, being well groomed. But you also have to get a little sneaky. What makes a producer happy? A segment that gets a lot of positive feedback. And that's where your friends can help. Enlist them for duty. Have them call or write the station saying how much they liked your bit. After a suitable waiting period, you can then put in a follow-up call to the station producer, proffering your services.

Now that you have got all the rules down, it's time for you to go out and get ready for your close-up! Lights, camera . . .

## Chapter Eight

# It Isn't Always about You!
*The Publicity Power of a
Charitable, Pro-social Agenda*

I AM NOT SAYING BILL AND MELINDA GATES DON'T BE-
lieve strongly in their work on behalf of AIDS research, or that the new Mrs. Paul McCartney is not
sincere about combating land mines. I have seen
how passionate Angelina Jolie is when it comes to
orphans, and let's face it, Michael J. Fox has a lot of
good reasons for being involved with the search
for a Parkinson's cure. But it's not always just good
intentions (or even tax write-offs) that motivate
celebrities to become philanthropists. The right
high-profile cause can be great PR, just the thing to
rehabilitate a slightly tainted reputation or to re-
gain the public's affection after a year of accusations
of greed, shoplifting, monopolistic business practices, adultery. One night Ben Affleck can be seen at

the card table playing celebrity poker; and the next day as the subject of a photo op visiting a terminally ill young fan in a local hospital. After a late night out in NYC at an after-hours club, it's not unusual for Leonardo DiCaprio's name to then be linked with a cause like breast cancer. And so on. True, celebrity golf tournaments and polo matches may seem like fun, as if they are simply providing playgrounds for the rich and famous to meet and greet each other, but the money they raise makes good charitable sense, too.

It's not only grave illnesses that make excellent causes celebres. In many towns and cities, lots of charitable work goes on in support of artistic and cultural institutions, and it is there that many society A-listers gather, whether for a costume ball at New York City's Metropolitan Museum or for a thousand-dollar-a-plate sit-down dinner to benefit a public library, zoo, or park. At events like these, socialites get the chance to mingle with Hollywood royalty and rising stars, and each brings a sort of cachet to the other. These occasions also give men and especially women the opportunity to don their most lavish designer fashions and pose for photographers from the newspapers, wire services, and magazines from around the world—glossy publications like *Town and*

*Country*, *Vanity Fair*, *Hamptons*, *Chicago* magazine, *Philadelphia* magazine, *Vogue*, *W*—the list is endless. The attendees just have to stand there and look gorgeous. They receive great publicity whose only cost is the price of a gown (which, in many cases, a designer probably provides) and the cost of the ticket (which is also probably provided free of charge to the major celebrities to get them to attend in the first place). It is an incestuous world, after all.

Couri Hay, who can always be counted on not only to know everything about everything but also to say something that's a little insightful and a little juicy and often a little bit snide, observes the following about climbing the social ladder, or breaking into the A-list: "Charity has always been the way in, whether it's a big town or a little town. Doing good is a way in."

Does this sound cynical? Remember that the descendants of the biggest and most ruthless American robber barons of past centuries have family names that today are more often associated with the charitable foundations they started than with the fact that they made their money exploiting workers and employing questionable business practices. And some of today's most highly regarded socialites have helped their more established neighbors to overlook their humble origins by picking the right charity to support, and then hanging on to their seat on its board for dear life.

As an example, take Dayssi Olarte de Kanavos, born in Colombia and raised in Queens, New York. She has managed to climb to the top New York social rungs by marrying a reasonably wealthy man (smile!), and then making the Sloan Kettering Cancer Memorial Fund her pet project. There and via other charitable activities, Dayssi befriended top socialites such as Nan Kempner and the Astors, as well as relative newcomers like the Trumps, and is now comfortably ensconced in the top tiers of New York society, where she wears her fabulous couture clothes at the glittering bashes she holds for her newly acquired friends.

When *New York Daily News* gossip columnist Lloyd Grove was still working the Washington, D.C., beat, he frequently wrote about socialite wannabe Kathy Kemper, a one-time tennis club pro Grove dubbed "Washington's Becky Sharp" (as in the protagonist of the novel *Vanity Fair*). It seems that out of her well-heeled tennis clientele sprang the seeds of a social circle, which gave her access to people with fame, money, power. She married a wealthy venture capitalist, and they started a charitable foundation.

Today she is a top Washington hostess who—mainly through her work with charities, including a tennis tournament that raises a good deal of money for a variety of worthy causes—is at the epicenter of social power there. Grove attributes her current stature to her networking and her charity work.

It's always been interesting to me that there is a pecking order within the world of charity work, and that it takes such a lot of ambition, strategy, and the right connections (not to mention money) to get to the top of it. In New York, it's ruled by people like Brooke Astor. In order to, say, run an important committee, according to Couri Hay, you have to "have a big enough name to attract the wannabes . . . they're always going to want your name on the committee." Hay says that in New York, and in the more sophisticated towns, "there are certain people who, through the right marriage or the right look, can fake it for a season or two," but who the real powers are always comes out in the end. (Hey! It really is just like in a Candace Bushnell novel!)

The bottom line is that aligning yourself with the right charity can legitimize you as a mover and shaker in the social world. If you are a criminal but you still have a big bank account, it can offer you redemption and rehabilitation. This really is one of those areas where you can still buy your way in, or your way back in. If you started life in Kew Gardens, Queens, or in Oakland, California, or in South Central Los Angeles—or in some plain, dull town out there—you can make the elite forget your humble beginnings with a few (quite a few) strategically donated dollars and membership on the right committees.

---

PAGE SIX has done many charity "exposés" but this one in 2000 was the most informative: "AL-MOST a year after PAGE SIX first revealed the Carol Baldwin Breast Cancer Fund paid for Mama Baldwin's car and Stony Brook apartment, *Forbes* magazine pans the charity for high overhead and low contribution to the cause.

"The foundation created by the mother of Alec, Billy, Daniel, and Steven spends more on fundraising than it does on research. *Forbes* found 58 percent of the charity's annual outlay of $570,000 went to overhead.

"The other four charities given bad marks by

*Forbes* are: the [Evander] Holyfield Foundation, the Ned Beatty Hope for Children Classic, the Magic Johnson Foundation, and the Nicole Brown Simpson Foundation.

"After the Baldwin charity was contacted by *Forbes*, it amended its income statements to shave off $123,000 from its expenses. Fund president Michael Maffetone tells Page Six the original filing was erroneous. 'It's the difference between what is tax-deductible and what is not,' he explained.

"The Baldwin fund's original financial statements for 1998, reported by *Forbes*, show $150,458 was spent on its golf tournament, and $45,611 for 'dinner gala expenses.' A mere $241,575 was handed over for breast cancer research grants, while $204,638 was left in the coffers for 1999.

"*Forbes* reports the charities run by Paul Newman, Elton John, Wolfgang Puck and Stephen King gave away more than 90 percent of their total outlays, keeping overhead in single digits.

"'Our standards call for charities to devote a bare minimum of 60 percent to charitable work, not to fundraising and overhead,' Dan Langan, spokesman for the National Charities Information Bureau, tells us."

━━━━━━━━━━━━━━━━━━━━━━━━━━━━━━━━

Sometimes it is crystal clear that a publicist has suggested to a celebrity with an ailing reputation that he or she take up the charity mantle. I doubt anyone thought that Michael Jackson's appearance on Capitol Hill to launch his AIDS in Africa endeavor came about organically. It is far more likely (I am just guessing here) that someone felt that he needed to give his fans something else to talk about other than whether it is legitimate for an adult male to sleep in the same bed with young boys. I also couldn't help feeling just a little bit skeptical when I found out that Jon Benet Ramsey's father has decided to run for political office. He was quoted as saying he wanted to give something back to all of the people who have supported him during the murder investigation of his daughter, but I wonder if there wasn't a publicist whispering in his ear.

There are many times, of course, when a celebrity's association with a cause or charity seems absolutely genuine and sincere. After all, why would Tim Robbins and Susan Sarandon keep pissing off powerful people by offering up their super-liberal political views if they didn't really believe in them? They are definitely not helping their careers here. I am also guessing that Sean Penn went to Iraq on his own steam, without consulting advisers. If not, perhaps he should consider getting new advisers.

When Bono and Paul O'Neill (former Bush Treasury Secretary) teamed up to tour Africa and to bring attention to the AIDS pandemic there, I am fairly sure their motives were, if not 100 percent pure, at least not designed to sell product. But the best application of charitable or other social or political work is when cause and motive just seem perfectly compatible, just seem right.

To me the best example of this is Newman's Own. How can you not love Paul Newman and Joanne Woodward? They are great actors, they're getting up there in years, they've had their fair share of triumphs but also of tragedies, and they are clearly people who not only don't take themselves too seriously but who also want to leave something behind after they're gone besides their acting legacies. Who could have predicted how successful a business Newman's Own would become, and therefore how astonishingly successful it's been as a way of raising money for charity? Recently, I noticed they've even branched out into dog food!

---

Check out your charity on www.guidestar.org. Look closely at its financials—every charity has to register with the IRS, and GuideStar will show you exactly how much money went to "overhead" (read: salaries or parties) and how much went to the actual benefit of the people it is supposed to benefit. Choose carefully! I suggest being part of an already established charity because the infrastructure (which can be costly and prohibitive) is already in place. Start your own if a) you are a huge star, b) you want to give back to the community in ways that are not being served, or c) you have a lot of money that can go into setting up a charity properly.

---

Another twist on bringing true sincerity and creativity to a good cause was Paul Simon's release of his *Graceland* record some years ago. He had come to love "world" music, especially African music. He didn't want just to borrow from that culture, though, and run laughing all the way to the bank.

Instead, he traveled to Africa, spending many, many months working with musicians there, eventually showcasing scores of African artists and their music in a way that also breathed new life into his own career.

Michael J. Fox and Christopher Reeve both have had to contend with severe health problems, Fox with Parkinson's and Reeve with spinal cord injury as a result of a horse-riding accident. They could easily have turned self-pitying or, out of vanity or pride, chosen not to allow their fans to see them in their vulnerable conditions. But both worked tirelessly to raise money for research into their respective conditions, hosting charity events, writing memoirs, doing media interviews to bring attention to the need for more financial contributions to these causes. In the process, they kept themselves in the public eye, and no doubt from sinking into the "why me?" depths. Days before his death, Christopher Reeve was, as usual, appearing in public, passionately making his case in support of stem cell research.

It's interesting to me that many of the rules of fame apply equally well to supporting a good cause or a charity. You need to do your homework and figure out what you're best at. If you're an accountant, then you can be the person to maintain the books, volunteer to be treasurer. If you are an interior decorator, you can help with event planning and decorations. If you are an office manager, your organizational skills and ability to plan ahead can be brought to bear.

You also need to get to know the media, figuring out who's looking for what and how you can get them to cover the party or benefit you're planning. Get the right people involved, so that the press wants to come out and write about your event. You need to know how to network, know how to look the part, know how to think strategically about advancing your cause.

Whether you're holding a silent auction to benefit a soup kitchen or, like Jimmy Carter, throwing your considerable influence behind a group like Habitat for Humanity, or just volunteering at the local nursing home, you are doing good work that will make you feel good—and at the same time, get yourself some good press!

## Chapter Nine

# Keeping the
# Momentum Going

ANDY WARHOL ONCE PREDICTED THAT EVERYONE WILL be famous for fifteen minutes. History is filled with those who lapped up their fifteen minutes before fading into oblivion. These include politicians who held office for one term and then were swept away by scandal or incompetence, or just because the public decided they liked someone else better; businessmen and women who got rich quickly but found staying on top much more difficult than getting there in the first place; countless artists, pop stars, and actors; and even those who achieve their brief fame not through an accomplishment or talent, but rather because of something sordid or shameful—remember John Bobbitt?

It's also true that there are people who have

achieved their stature through their work or their talent or their beauty, but who then make a misstep and become forever defined not by their prior accomplishments but by their mistakes. Is there anyone who will remember Gary Condit for his record in the House of Representatives rather than for his affair with Chandra Levy? Can you think of Farrah Fawcett now without thinking of her meltdown on *Late Night* with David Letterman? Okay, it's debatable as to whether Janet Jackson's nipple-gate was a mistake or a PR stunt, but are you going to think first of her music and then of her Super Bowl shenanigans, or the other way around? Bill Clinton will no doubt spend the rest of his life trying to be sure that history books focus on his achievements as president rather than on his dabblings with an intern. Is the first thing you remember about Gary Hart the fact that he was photographed on a yacht called the *Monkey Business* with a woman other than his wife on his lap? Or that Rob Lowe was best known prior to his role on *The West Wing* for his starring role in a homemade porn video?

As tough as it is to break into the big time, whether it's in television, movies, politics, music, or business, it is much more difficult to sustain success and fame over time. It takes good luck, good judgment, and a lot of skill to stay on top, and those who have managed to do it know that the hard work really begins *after* you've made it.

So what can you learn from the masters? Now that you've gotten your name into print, gotten your new venture up and running, gotten your first acting role, cut your first record, gotten yourself onto that charity committee you've been angling for, how do you make sure you don't totally screw it up?

### 1. Don't take anything for granted.

Earlier in the book, some of the top publicists in the business talked about some of their biggest clients, and how the real superstars work hard to be gracious, to earn their reputations and their paychecks every day, to give back a little—even a lot.

So often I have seen played out that old maxim that the bigger they are, the harder they fall. Just as the press and public love having a hand in building someone up, we seem equally delighted in having a hand in bringing that person down, if the opportunity presents itself, particularly if on their way up the ladder they have not seemed sufficiently grateful.

For example, a lot of people feel that Russell Crowe will have a hard time ever winning another Oscar, even if he deserves it, because he has so frequently behaved badly in public (and because he so publicly jilted one-time America's sweetheart Meg Ryan). (Perhaps Russell Crowe should find himself a charity to embrace!) Colin Farrell seemed like he had it all when he appeared on all those magazine covers right after his fantastic role as Danny Wentworth in *Minority Report*. But then every time he appeared in public he seemed drunk and disorderly, and he always seemed to be behaving like a cad towards the multitudes of women he was dating. He is in danger of becoming a cliché. Courtney Love is another scary example of fame and talent run amok. In a few short years she went from rock royalty during her marriage to Kurt Cobain and the glory days of Hole to makeover triumph (remember when she started to dress in clothes that weren't "slut rock"?), and then to whatever the opposite of "Mother of the Year" is.

Gossip columnists—I hate to admit this but it's true—feed on this kind of reversal of fortune. We are all too ready to take our knives out, waiting for Britney to vomit in public or for Winona to get caught shoplifting. Perhaps some of this is because there's actually a lot of things we know that we can't print—we either don't have strong-enough confirmations to go to press with a story even though we've heard the rumors again and again, or a publicist or stage mother or record executive or SOMEONE has begged us for a favor, and therefore we've had to sit on something that is so tempting, so juicy . . .

It may seem that a few big names like Nicole Kidman, Renée Zellweger, Tom Hanks, Steve Martin, Robin Williams (okay, he is still living down the fact that he left his wife to marry the nanny)—some of the real class acts out there—get all the positive media coverage they do because they're so successful that no one can touch them. WRONG! These stars are gracious, hardworking professionals who are courteous and responsive. They not only know what it takes to remain at the top of their games but also know that their status doesn't exempt them from having to play by the rules; instead, it makes it so that they will always be scrutinized more closely because they're in the big time, which means they'd better be exemplary in their behavior and have trustworthy publicists who can help

them out when they make the inevitable minor in-
fractions.

For most of us, it would seem pretty great being
Jennifer Aniston and Brad Pitt—gorgeous, rich, tons
of friends, apparently crazy in love. On the other
hand, though, they can't go shopping for furniture
without causing a small riot. Their marriage is constantly being poked and prodded for weaknesses.
There is continuous and intense speculation about
their sex life (are they not doing it enough, and is
that why it's taken her so long to get pregnant? is he
doing it with Angelina Jolie?). And yet these two always have smiles on their faces and never complain
(as so many do) about the difficulties of celebrity.
They know that they are among the privileged few,
and they know what it takes to remain in that select
company.

So what's the advice you can take away from this?
Just because you think you've "made it" doesn't
mean you are assured a place on the top of the heap.
Surround yourself with smart, honest people who
are unafraid to tell you when you are behaving like
a jerk. Always be thankful for what you have, and
know that all the hard work it took to get you there
is still necessary once you've achieved your goal.

Martha Stewart is an incredibly smart and talented woman who alienated a few too many people along the way, and some say that she paid for it with a guilty verdict.

## 2. Cultivate grace under pressure.

To me, Karen "Duff" Duffy epitomizes this concept. She is one of the most beautiful women on the planet, was one of the original MTV v-js, a Revlon model, an actress, and dated some of the hottest guys out there, including George Clooney and Dwight Yoakum.

However, several years ago she was diagnosed with a serious illness that is often fatal, the symptoms of which are excruciatingly painful. In *Model Patient*, the book she wrote about her condition, she describes the lengths she went to in order to keep up her own spirits during the worst of the illness, and to keep up the spirits of her friends and family at the same time. She didn't sit around asking, "Why me?", though she was certainly more than entitled to do so. Today, many years after her original diagnosis, she lives uncomplainingly with her symptoms. She has a great marriage, recently became a mother, and has a thriving career as a writer and TV personality. But the thing that is inescapable about her is that she is a fearless person and dispenses the best advice of pretty much anyone I can think of. Her mantra is to take the high road whenever possible, to surprise your detractors not with your anger but with your ability to rise above the fray. Grace under pressure, indeed.

### 3. Use the power of reinvention.

I only need to say one word here: Madonna. I don't know how popular this forty-five-year-old is with the teenybopper set, but she certainly is holding her own! Madonna is a genius about her image. When the frosted hair and "Like a Virgin" phase seemed to be in danger of playing itself out, she got buff, went platinum, and started her dominatrix phase, leaving behind bad boy Sean Penn and taking up with ultrasophisticated older guy Warren Beatty. Then came her entrepreneur/queen phase, when it seemed her image was almost entirely based on her ability to control her career, to build an empire. She became a mother but seemed to have no use for her daughter's father except as sperm donor. She entered a new phase when she met and married Guy Ritchie, moved to England, and had another child. She wrote children's books and promoted them in lady bountiful outfits. She found Kabbalah, and enlisted high profile friends from Gwyneth Paltrow to Demi Moore to join her, becoming a sort of spiritual earth mother. During each new phase she adopted a new fashion style, thereby maintaining her place in the fashion magazines. It no longer seems to matter if her records hit #1 or if her movies are hits. She is an icon.

Demi Moore is another example of someone who has completely changed her image, successfully reviving a career that had seemed dead. In an earlier incarnation, of course, she was known for her hard-driving career moves, her marriage to Bruce Willis, and of course for her seething ambition (including a willingness to get naked for *Vanity Fair* while very pregnant, as well as to shave her head or bulk up like Arnold Schwarzenegger). Then there were several movies in a row that bombed, and she seemed to withdraw completely from the scene.

SHE'S BAAAAAACK!! She produced the Austin Powers movies from high atop her Idaho retreat. She then agreed to a small but high profile acting role in the *Charlie's Angels* sequel. Before the film even came out she started doing a little publicity here and there, looking absolutely gorgeous with her impossibly fit forty-year-old body and shiny hair.

Then Ashton Kutcher came along, and suddenly once again she was the hottest star going, even though she hadn't starred in anything for years. Talk about reinventing yourself!

Take my word for it—she is the envy of every forty-plus woman out there, and is single-handedly changing the way twenty-something guys think about their mothers' friends . . .

One thing you have to say for Bob Dylan: Even he knows how to reinvent himself. Granted, he is still singing pretty much the same songs as at the start of his career, and he looks pretty much the same (though his voice has got to be about three octaves higher). But by teaming up with people like Sheryl Crow, or agreeing to appear in a Victoria's Secret commercial, you have to admit he is showing how he can mix it up!

### 4. *Keep proving how good you are at what you do—and keep your integrity.*

Senator John McCain is an extraordinary public figure. Whether you're a Democrat or a Republican, you can't help admiring the guy. While so many senators are doing little and sounding pompous about it, McCain has every reason to act like he has all the answers, and yet he always comes across as direct and honest, and displays a lot of humility, and it's not fake humility either. He was a prisoner of war, but he doesn't pull that out of his pocket whenever it's convenient. His literary agent, Flip Brophy, president of Sterling Lord Literistic, says that she is constantly astonished at how down-to-earth he is, how responsive he is to the people who need him to do things for them, how infrequently he falls into "Politician-Speak." "He really is that man you see on television, offering thoughtful, un-self-serving honest views," she says. "What you see is what you get, which is why he has become such a hero." That's one way of staying on top!

Or look at Phil Jackson. Every team that guy touches turns to gold. Why? I read somewhere that when he took over as coach of the Los Angeles Lakers, he gave each team member a different book to read, one that spoke to what he saw as that player's own greatest strengths and challenges. He views his job as being more than just a basketball coach. He sees his players as whole people, as spiritual beings as well as athletes, a view that stems from his Zen Buddhist beliefs. Whether you believe that this is crap or that he is sincere, the point is that it works. Not only is he about the winningest coach in NBA history, but he is cited in many top business management books for his leadership skills.

Diane Sawyer also comes to mind when I think of people who are great at what they do, and also great at staying on top. At the start of her career, a lot of people saw Diane Sawyer as just another pretty face, a talking head. She would probably agree that it was her looks that initially gave her a leg up—she did win a beauty pageant, after all—but who would have guessed that her next move would be to work as a researcher/writer for President Nixon? Working in the White House gave her chops, a sort of credibility she might have otherwise lacked. As a television journalist, she has been tireless. She is famous for being prepared, for never resting on her laurels, for still being hungry for the big story. Still, she is a wonderful, friendly, down-to-earth person, who always shows a sense of humor about herself and the world around her. She is an engaged participant in the goings on in New York City, and is always ready, despite her early work hours, to lend her hand and her name to a variety of causes. Not to mention that she and husband Mike Nichols seem like a completely devoted couple, and that she is viewed as one of America's most fashionable women. GO, DIANE!

## 5. *When all else fails, get yourself a reality show.*

Donald Trump must have been born under a lucky star (though he also has fantastic marketing instincts and is a shrewd businessman). On more than one occasion people have pronounced him broke, washed up, or just hopelessly unhip, comb-over hairdo and all.

For years he has been central to New York's social scene, and of course he is one of the people responsible for revitalizing Atlantic City. But with NBC's *The Apprentice*, he has once again come to the front and center of the mainstream with his big personality and his hirings and firings.

Look at Jessica and Nick, or Sharon and Ozzy. There may be a time when these people will fade from the public consciousness, will not be so ubiquitous, won't seem to be everywhere, visible every time we turn around. But for now, reality television has made them huge. If your career, your business, or your reputation is beginning to wane, I can get you Mark Burnett's phone number. Just don't call me at deadline time to ask for it.

### 6. *Patience is a virtue.*

When I look at some of the people out there who have the most staying power, I think not only of the long, hard hours they've put in, but also of all the storms they've weathered, how many times they've been up and down. It's true that for most of these folks, the downs have not taken them all the way down, nor have they lasted very long, but no one is the flavor of the month every month for their entire career.

Look at Larry King. Once considered the king of the softball interview on a minor cable channel, he is now the go-to guy for every big story, every big celebrity out there.

Love her or hate her, Suzanne Somers is the only woman I know who can make menopause sound like it's actually a time to look forward to—hell, she's having more sex now than Hugh Hefner. Or think of Anna Wintour, editor of *Vogue*. She really didn't have to wait that long to see her arch-rival

Tina Brown go through three magazines, and then leave the industry behind her—while Anna herself sails on, as serene and well-coiffed as ever.

Don't worry, Tom Cruise—you'll get your Oscar one of these days. Just be patient.

Thank you to my friends and family, Leigh Haber, Todd Shuster, the boys of PAGE SIX and the *New York Post,* the folks at Miramax Books and all who contributed to this book, either with interviews or otherwise . . . I appreciate it with all my heart.